MOORS IN AMERICA

A COMPILATION

BY

SIS. TAUHEEDAH S. NAJEE-ULLAH EL
&
BRO. VICTOR TAYLOR EL

FOR THE EDUCATION AND ENLIGHTENMENT OF
THE MOORISH AMERICAN COMMUNITY

© 2014, 2020

A Moorish Guide Publishing Company
califamedia.com
All Rights, Remedies & Liberties Reserved

Black & White Student's Edition

CONTENTS

1. The Great Cover Up 4
2. Who Was Found In Da Mounds 23
3. Moors And The American Revolution 31
4. Digging For The Red Roots 44
5. The Unholy Days We Celebrate 84
6. Black Indians/ Moors 86
7. Black/ Moors In The Confederacy 101
8. White Slavery And The Moors 118
9. Islam Before Columbus And During The Antebellum America 127
10. Other Moorish/ Black Facts 152

The Great Meeting Is On!
BREAKING THE CHAINS OF SLAVERY:
THE MOORS' RISE FROM CIVIL DEATH

Noble Drew Ali, Founder of
The Moorish Science Temple of America
Chicago, IL., U.S.A.

The Great Cover Up

Who are the first people to inhabit the land commonly known as North, South, and Central America? Since 1928 the answer to this question has been hidden — but not withheld— from mainstream America.

Displace and blacked out though white-wash, the covering up of the anthropological and scientific facts of Americas original people being what are today commonly known as "black people."

AMERICA: LAND OF THE MOORS

Archaeological Cover-Ups?

"Who controls the past, controls the future.

Who controls the present, controls the past."

George Orwell, *1984*

by David Hatcher Childress
World Explorers Club
403 Kemp Street
Kempton, Illinois 60946-0074 USA
Tel: (815) 253 6390
Fax: (815) 253 6300

Most of us are familiar with the last scene in the popular Indiana Jones archaeological-adventure film *Raiders of the Lost Ark* in which an important historical artefact, the Ark of the Covenant from the Temple in Jerusalem, is locked in a crate and put in a giant warehouse, never to be seen again, thus ensuring that no history books will have to be rewritten and no history professor will have to revise the lecture that he has been giving for the last forty years.

While the film was fiction, the scene in which an important ancient relic is buried in a warehouse is uncomfortably close to reality for many researchers. To those who investigate allegations of archaeological cover-ups, there are disturbing indications that the most important archaeological institute in the United States, the Smithsonian Institution, an independent federal agency, has been actively suppressing some of the most interesting and important archaeological discoveries made in the Americas.

The Vatican has been long accused of keeping artefacts and ancient books in their vast cellars, without allowing the outside world access to them. These secret treasures, often of a controversial historical or religious nature, are allegedly suppressed by the Catholic Church because they might damage the church's credibility, or perhaps cast their official texts in doubt. Sadly, there is overwhelming evidence that something very similar is happening with the Smithsonian Institution.

The Smithsonian Institution was started in 1829 when an eccentric British millionaire by the name of James Smithson, died and left $515,169 to create an institution "for the increase and diffusion of knowledge among men." Unfortunately, there is evidence the Smithsonian has been more active in the suppression of knowledge rather than the diffusion of it for the last hundred years.

The cover-up and alleged suppression of archaeological evidence began in late 1881 when John Wesley Powell, the geologist famous for exploring the Grand Canyon, appointed Cyrus Thomas as the director of the Eastern Mound Division of the Smithsonian Institution's Bureau of Ethnology.

When Thomas came to the Bureau of Ethnology he was a "pronounced believer in the existence of a race of Mound Builders, distinct from the American Indians." However, John Wesley Powell, the director of the Bureau of Ethnology, a very sympathetic man toward the American Indians, had lived with the peaceful Winnebago Indians of Wisconsin for many years as a youth and felt that American Indians were unfairly thought of as primitive and savage.

The Smithsonian began to promote the idea that Native Americans, at that time being exterminated in the Indian Wars, were descended from advanced civilisations and were worthy of respect and protection. They also began a program of suppressing any archaeological evidence that lent credence to the school of thought known as Diffusionism, a school which believes that throughout history there has been widespread dispersion of culture and civilisation via contact by ship and major trade routes.

The Smithsonian opted for the opposite school, known as Isolationism. Isolationism holds that most civilisations are isolated from each other and that there has been very little contact between them, especially those that are separated by bodies of water. In this intellectual war that started in the 1880s, it was held that even contact between the civilisations of the Ohio and Mississippi Valleys was rare, and certainly these civilisations did not have any contact with such advanced cultures as the Mayas, Toltecs, or Aztecs in Mexico and Central America. By Old World standards this is an extreme, and even ridiculous idea, considering that the river system reached to the Gulf of Mexico and these civilisations were as close as the opposite shore of the gulf. It was like saying that cultures in the Black Sea area could not have had contact with the Mediterranean.

When the contents of many ancient mounds and pyramids of the Midwest were examined, it was shown that the history of the Mississippi River Valleys was that of an ancient and sophisticated culture that had been in contact with Europe and other areas. Not only that, the contents of many mounds revealed burials of huge men, sometimes seven or eight feet tall, in full armour with swords and sometimes huge treasures.

For instance, when Spiro Mound in Oklahoma was excavated in the 1930s, a tall man in full armour was discovered along with a pot of thousands of pearls and other artefacts, the

OH LORD, WHEN WILL THE SLEEPING GIANT AWAKE, OR WILL HE EVER?

1 Cor: 3:16 - KNOW YOU NOT THAT YOUR ARE THE TEMPLR OF GOD, AND THAT THE SPIRIT OF GOD DWELLETH IN YOU?

Ps. 82:6 - I HAVE SAID YOU ARE GOD AND ALL OF YOU ARE CHILDREN OF THE MOST HIGH

JONH 10:34 - IS IT NOT WRITTEN IN YOUR LAW, THAT I SAID YOU ARE GODS?

BLACK AMERICA B.C TO A.D. STOLEN LEGACY II

Most convincing of the presence of Africans in the New World is, of course, the famous colossal stone head of Tres Zapotes No. 2, not only on account of its purely negroid features, but even more so by its typically Ethiopian braided pigtails, endings in rings and tassels. This head first appears in recent times in *Nile Valley Civilizations*, edited by Van Sertima. It has been seldom displayed among the other Olmec heads.

Alexander von Wuthenau
African Presence in Early America

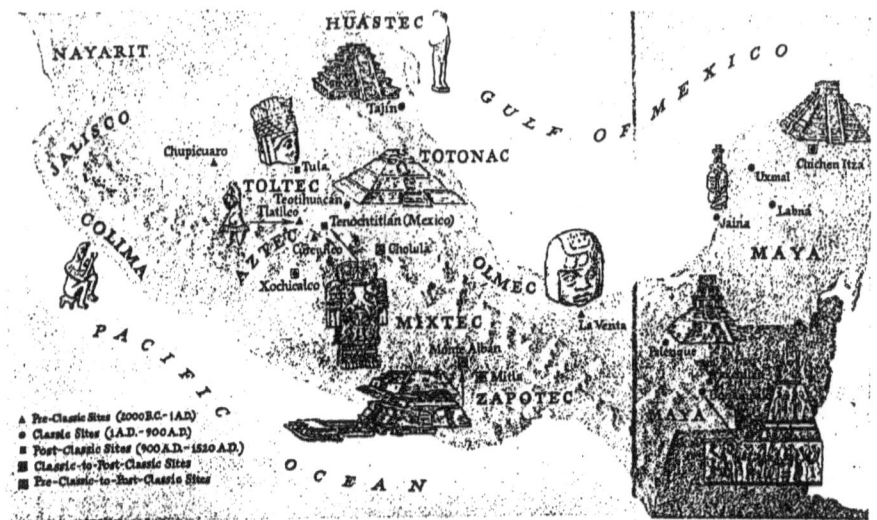

REMNANTS OF THE PAST, the buildings and objects above are among the most notable creations of pre-Hispanic Mexico. The names in brown represent various important Mexican cultures, and are placed in the regions where each flourished. Smaller type indicates major archeological sites where remains have been found. At top is the Totonac Niche-Pyramid located at Tajín; other religious sites include the Pyramid of the Sun at Teotihuacán, the remains of the religious center at Monte Albán, the Temple of Kukulkan at Chichen Itzá, Palenque's Temple of the Sun, and the fre... ampák. Ceramic and stone figures are foun... coasts of the Gulf of Mexico and the Pacific statue of Coatlicue, a terrible death goddess, in the vicinity of the main square of today's b...

never become known. The Spaniards, in their zeal both to subjugate and Christianize the New World, systematically set about destroying buildings, cities, works of art, pictographic records, everything they could find that was indicative of the level that the primitive Americans had achieved. What is known of ancient Mexico has been determined from fragments—the ruins of temples and cities (much of Mex-

revision and correction as new archeological sites are found and excavated. It is believed that Mexico contains at least 10,000 such sites still unexplored.

One of the earliest cultures, the so-called Olmec, flourished in the tropical lowlands of Veracruz where its traces are found in giant sculptured heads with moonlike faces and thick lips—a style that found its way into other early

and Mitla. To the east and farther s... are the ruins of the various Mayan civ... The architecture in all cases is startl... ative of modern design in its arran... mass, space and form, whether built... or adobe, with or without mortar, wi... arches or flat roofs. Everywhere th... dence of a highly developed aestheti... stone sculpture, ceramic work, the...

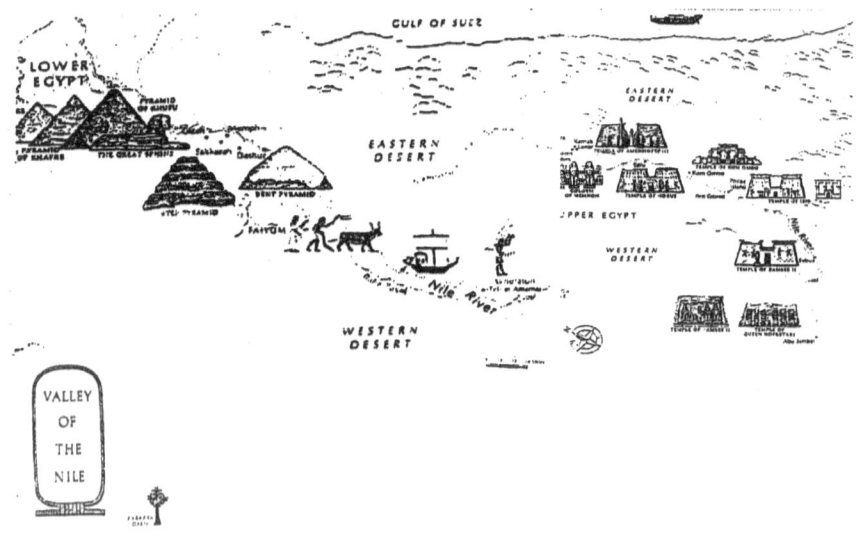

Attention Mexicans:

This is the root of your history, its cradle and its altar. Listen to the most silent voices of the most ancient culture in Mexico, the mother of the civilization of our continent. The Olmecs converted rain into harvest, the sun into a calendar, stone into sculpture, cotton into cloth, pilgrimage into commerce, mountains into thrones, jaguars into religion and men into gods.

This incredible sculpture, with distinctive African features, was said to have been carved around 1100 B.C.E. It was discovered in Tres Zapotes and is now on display in San Andre's Tuxtla, Veracruz, Mexico.

OLMEC

BLACK AMERICA B.C TO A.D. STOLEN LEGACY II

The Olmec lived in Mesoamerica. The Mesoamerican Culture Area, or Middle America, comprises much of present-day Mexico as well as the northern part of Central America. In the centuries before Europeans reached the Americas, Mesoamerica was the most densely populated region, with many different Indian cultures. *Olmec* (pronounced OL-mek), also written as *Olmeca*, is a term derived from the rubber trees growing in the area and applied by scholars to the cultures.

Scholars believe the Olmec established the "mother civilization" of Mesoamerica. That is to say, their culture influenced other cultures that followed. From about 1200 B.C. to A.D. 300, Olmec culture dominated the region.

Sometimes the period when the Olmec dominated Mesoamerica is referred to as the Preclassic period. Then came the Classic period, when the MAYA flourished. Then followed the Postclassic period, when the TOLTEC and AZTEC flourished. (In the study of PRE-HISTORIC INDIANS north of Mesoamerica, however, these three periods together are usually called the Formative period.)

The Olmec homeland was situated mainly along the Gulf coast to the east of present-day Mexico City. Yet the Olmec had extensive trade contacts all over Mesoamerica. On finding Olmec objects at sites far from the Gulf coast, archaeologists are sometimes uncertain if the ancient inhabitants were actually Olmec or were other Indians who obtained Olmec objects in trade.

The Olmec carved giant heads from basalt, a type of volcanic rock. Some of these were as heavy as 20 tons, with helmet-like headdresses. The Olmec traveled far to obtain the basalt to make these mammoth sculptures. To transport the rock, they dragged it overland and floated it on rafts. The Olmec also traveled great distances to get jade to make statues, the mineral magnetite to make

Olmec mammoth basalt head-statue

Olmec Head

Xalapa, Mexico, ca. 200 B.C.-A.D. 200. Dating back to 1200 B.C., The Olmec civilization was the earliest civilization in the Americas. This culture is best known for the gigantic carved stone heads, such as this example, which measures a colossal eight feet in height. They are believed to be the portraits of Olmec kings. *http://www.dl.ket.org/humanities/sculpt/olmec.fwx*

A Negroid Olmec sculpture carved in jade. Mexico cir. 1150 B.C.

ing copper imported from the north. They fashioned intricate copper luxury items, including beads, bracelets, rings, gorgets (ornamental collars), and axes. At one site, a twenty-eight pound (thirteen-kilogram) ceremonial copper ax was found.

Many Adena sites were ruined in the nineteenth century by amateur archaeologists who looted them for their artifacts. Unknown numbers of others have been destroyed by U.S. land-use practices, including highway construction, urban sprawl, mechanized agriculture, and inundation by reservoirs. Early non-Indian homesteaders in the region showed little interest in the mounds, and very little was done to either protect them or study them systematically before many of them had been destroyed.

It is not known whether the Hopewell Culture, which succeeded the Adena Culture, was the result of the migration of new people into the region, or whether the Hopewell people were the descendants of the Adena. The two existed side by side for a time, so a case can be made either that Adena Culture gradually evolved into Hopewell Culture, with the changes taking place at different rates in different places, or that the Hopewellians were a different people who gradually supplanted the Adena.

— D. L. Birchfield

SEE ALSO:
Hopewell Culture; Mississippian Culture; Mound Builders; Serpent Mound.

AFRICAN-AMERICANS

The term *African-American* and its closely related predecessor *Afro-American* have both been used to refer to people of African or part-African ancestry living in the Americas and especially in the United States. Generally, the term *African-American* is used to describe people descended from the brown-skinned peoples of Africa, those who also call themselves Black or Black Americans, and not for those descended from the lighter-colored peoples, of some parts of North Africa, such as Algeria or Morocco, which are considered Arab nations. The term never seems to be used for people born in Africa with European ancestry, such as white people from South Africa,

A collection of ancient Olmec funerary figures, from Mexico's Natural Museum of Anthropology. Artifacts such as these, with human figures bearing ethnic features that have been described as African, have led some scholars to speculate about the possibility of early African explorations of the Americas.

The Phoenician at home and abroad retained his characteristic high-crowned hat, the *hennin*, worn on formal occasions. It is here illustrated by two terracotta figurines. Left, an American example, excavated from a Mound Builder burial mound. Right, a figurine from Hagia Irene, Cyprus Museum. Both figurines date from the 8th to 6th century B.C. For a comparison of the alphabets used by the Phoenician colonists in Iowa and in southern Spain, see page 162. From S. D. Peet, *The Mound Builders*, 1892.

The Libyan colonists introduced into North America not only distinctively North African art styles and language, but also representations of African animals. The African elephant, carved to form a pipe-bowl, is one of several similar examples from Iowa; when originally found in the Davenport mounds and in the neighboring areas, they were taken to be mastodons, and later dismissed as modern

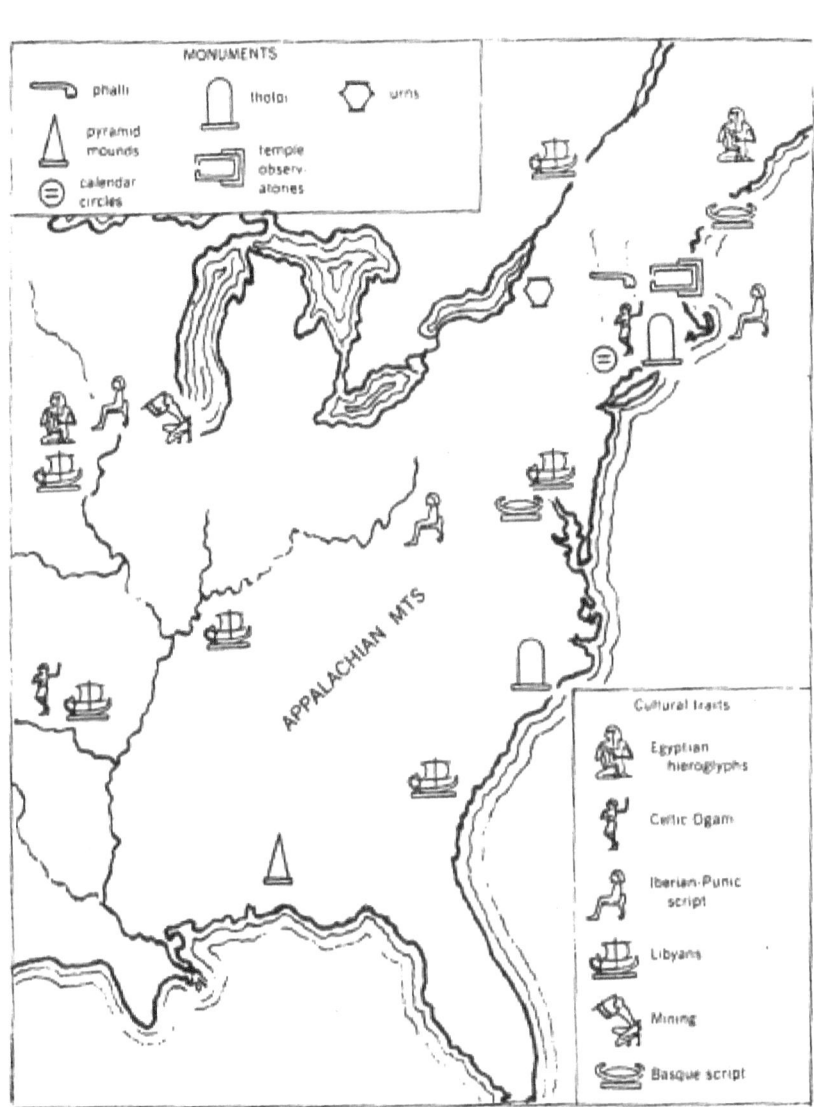

European and North African cultural interfaces and colonies, circa 800 B.C. For sailing routes, see map on pages 106–107.

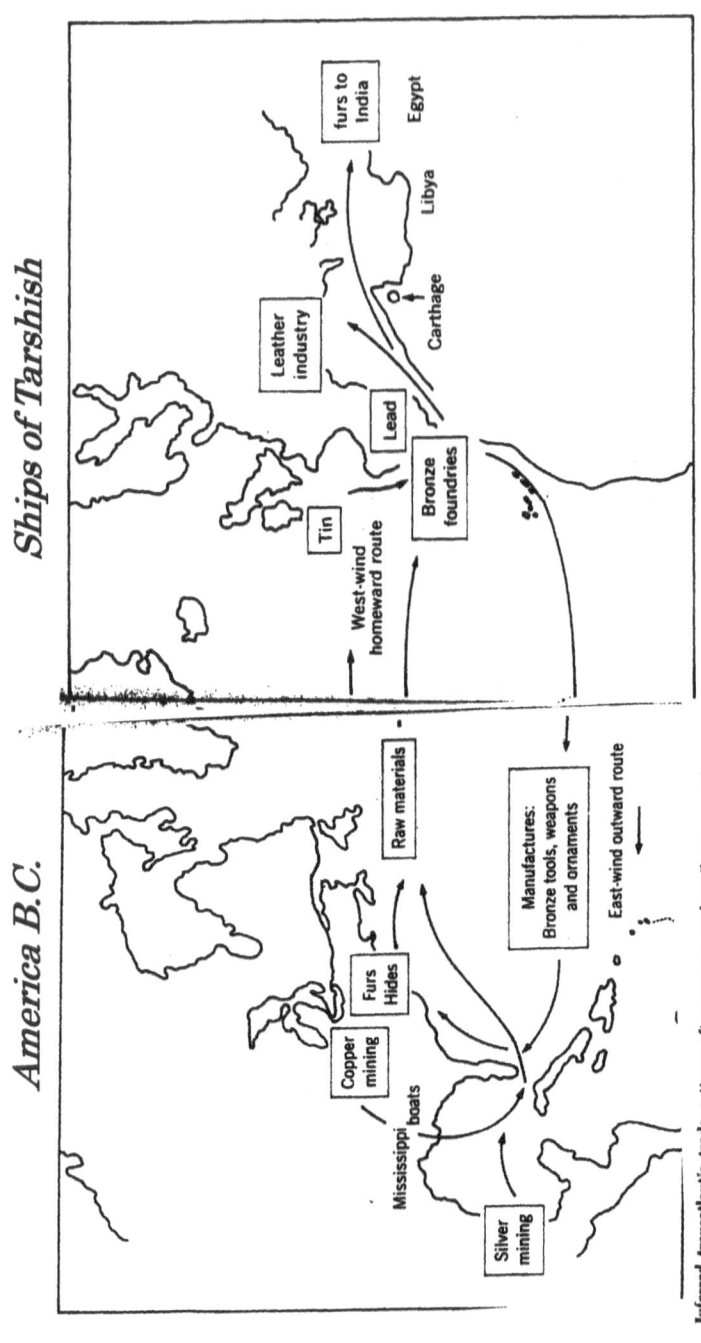

America B.C.

Ships of Tarshish

Inferred transatlantic trade patterns after 500 B.C. and until 179 B.C. The conquest of Egypt by Darius I in 525 B.C. and the successive rise of the Greek and Roman empires effectively closed the eastern Mediterranean to Carthaginian shipping. Carthage retaliated by closing the Straits of Gibraltar to all European mariners. Under the guise of supposed Spanish and North African trade, Carthaginian merchants exploited the North Atlantic resources, bringing to Cadiz the copper of the Celtiberian settlements of North America, and the tin of Cornwall, to provide the raw materials of a bronze industry, whose products were re-exported to Britain, Gaul, North America, and West Africa. The Celts of New England obtained a share of the American imports by supplying furs and hides, both of which the Carthaginians re-exported to the eastern Mediterranean as supposed products of Gaul, the furs even reaching India. By the time the Romans conquered Spain and Carthage they had adequate alternate sources of these materials, and they took no interest in overseas shipping, having no merchant navy. The North American trade dwindled, the last phases presumably being operated by the maritime Celts of Brittany until their conquest by Caesar in 55 B.C. For 400 years after the Battle of Actium in 31 B.C. the Romans had no navy, since they had no rivals, and the memory of America apparently was lost. By 200 A.D. geographers believed that a voyage westward from Spain would lead to India and China, and this was the inheritance of Columbus.

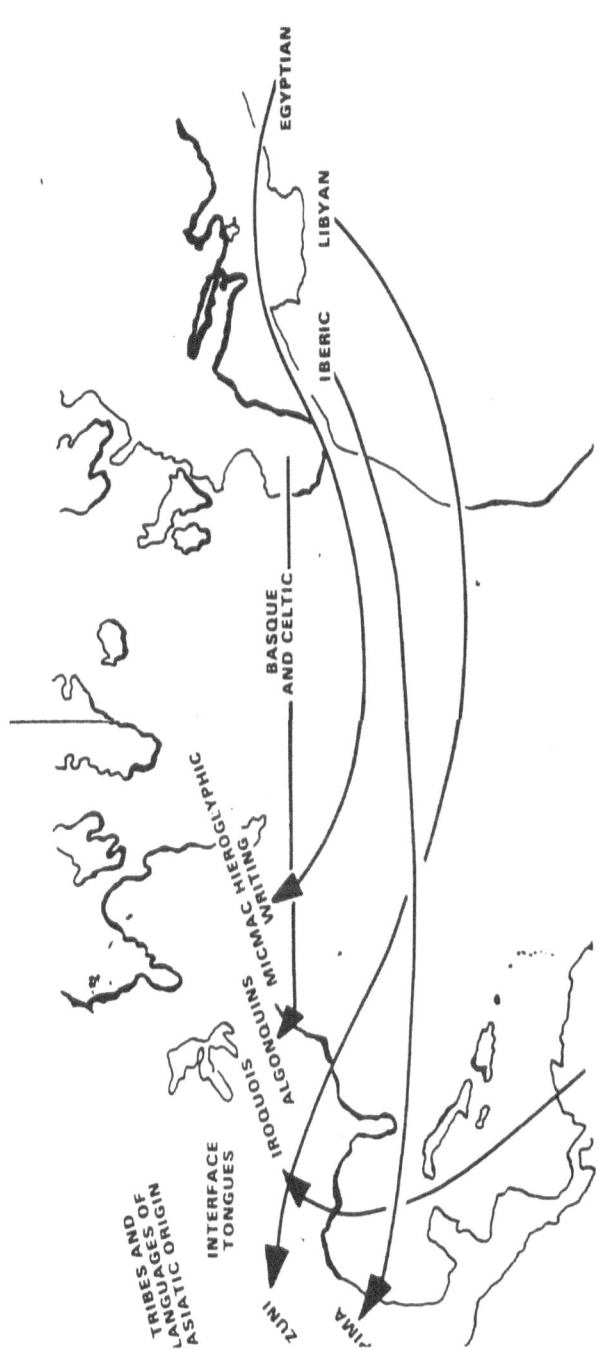

The cultural heritage of the Amerindian peoples is reflected in the co linguistic relationships of the spoken languages today. Only a few of many are illustrated above. The earliest languages came from Asia, via the west and there has been a continuing input of Asiatic words from the Pacific peated incursions have taken place. On the Atlantic side ancient Libyan, Eg Phoenician, Celtic, and Basque colonists brought dialects of which some d dant tongues can still be recognized. Incursions from the south added Iro while some Norse speech entered the Algonquian area from the northeast.

THE AFRICAN ORIGIN OF THE ALPHABET

The Phoenicians (Punic) colonists of Iowa used an alphabet that shows clearly that their homeland was in the Iberian peninsula. The Iowa inscription was found at Davenport in 1874, and is written in the Iberian alphabet whose sound values were determined in Spain 60 years later. Failure to identify the Iowa alphabet led archeologists until now to suppose that the Davenport finds were fraudulent.

Some more exampl[es of] hieroglyphs, the form [of which was] Maillard in 1738 and continued until his death in 1762. A preliminary study suggests that several thousand of the Micmac hieroglyphs are derived from Egyptian models. As the modern decipherment of Egyptian began only in 1797, when Zoega deduced the meaning "name" for the cartouche sign, it is evident that the Micmac hieroglyphs must already have been transmitted to North America more than 2000 years ago, when they were still in use in Egypt.

meaning	formal or Palace style of Egypt	informal or hieratic style of Egypt	hieratic style of Iowa
the god Osiris			
the New Year Festival			
sunrise			
stone			
illuminated			
priest			
Star-watcher			

Examples illustrating the script styles employed in the formal hieroglyphic inscriptions of public monuments in ancient Egypt, the hieratic or informal script of ancient Egypt, and the hieratic style of the Davenport stele of Iowa. Use of the spiral sign in place of the chicken symbol for the sound W points to a date later than about 1400 B.C., and the presence of Iberian and Libyan script on the same stele probably brings the date to about 800–700 B.C. This would correspond to the XXII (Libyan) Dynasty of Egypt, at which epoch it is likely that Libyan Pharaohs would encourage distant voyages. The priest who inscribed the tablet, whose name seems to have been Star-watcher, probably accompanied a mainly Libyan expedition that established a colony in Iowa by sailing up the Mississippi River.

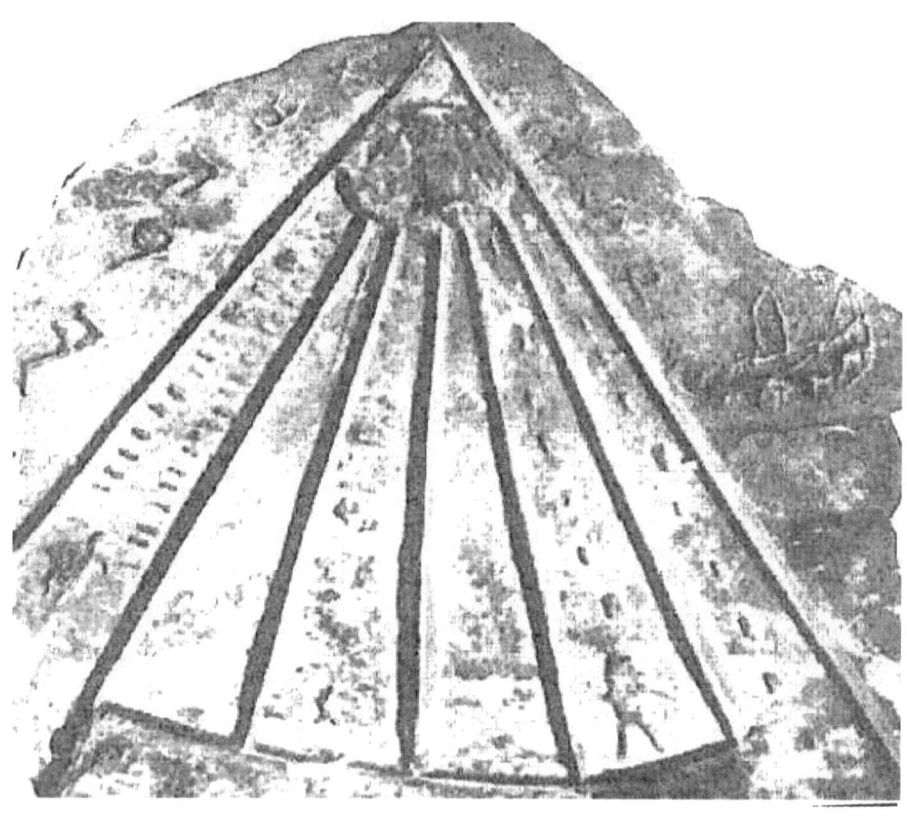

The Pontotoc stele, found in Oklahoma, is apparently the work of an early Iberian colonist in America, as the script is that known otherwise only from the Cachao-da-Rapa region in northern Portugal. It depicts the life-giving rays of the sun descending upon the earth beneath. To the left the Iberian Punic letters spell "Start of dawn," to the right "Dusk," with the crescent-ship of the moon. Two of the panels contain Ogam Punic, partly illegible, but sufficiently clear to disclose the phrases "When Baal-Ra rises in the east, the beasts are content, and (when he hides his face) they are displeased." These identify the inscription as an extract from the *Hymn to the Aton* by Pharaoh Akhnaton, here translated into Iberian Punic. Further study of this remarkable stele is still in progress. Although Akhnaton's hymn dates from the thirteenth century B.C., this American version can scarcely be older than about 800 B.C. The engraver was interrupted, covered over his work with soil, and never returned to complete the blank panels. *Gloria Farley, Weldon W. Stout*

The builders of the original Hopewell Mounds appear initially to have been mainly Libyans. In classical times Libyans were still for the most part an olive-skinned European stock, of mixed Anatolian, Greek, and Berber derivation, speaking an adoptive language of the Egyptian group, though retaining also many words of Anatolian and Greek origin. The appearance of negroid types in the sculpture of the mounds, however, indicates that many crew members of the Libyan ships must have been Nubians, and that as time went by they intermarried with the Libyans. This head, from Seip Mound, Ohio, exemplifies the Nubian stock. The Nubians probably introduced the high style of sculptured African animals, soon adapted to form pipe bowls as the colonists adopted the Amerindian predilection for tobacco. So far as is known (in 1976) the Nubian hieroglyphic alphabet was not one of the imports, and indeed the Hopewellian culture seems quite early to have become illiterate. This might reflect a "slave revolt," in which the few literate aristocrats were eliminated.

2. *Dentals* (consonants made against the teeth).
    a. African d becomes Zuni t, as in African *dessew* (shrine) and Zuni *teshqi* (shrine).
    b. African t equals Zuni t, as in African *ta* (flat land) and Zuni *ta* (flat land).
3. *Palatals* (consonants made against the palate).
    a. African ch equals Zuni ch, as in African *chme* (sow seed) and Zuni *chima* (sow wheat).
    b. African ch can also become Zuni k or sh, as in African *chol* (honeycomb) and Zuni *kali* (honeycomb).
4. *Velars* (consonants made in the throat).
    a. African g becomes Zuni ch, as in African *gaba* (assemble) and Zuni *chapa* (assemble).
    b. African K becomes Zuni k or q, as in African *koe* (place) and Zuni *kwe* (place).
5. *Liquid sonants* ("tongued humming").
    African l and r become Zuni l or lh, as in African *lol* (bed) and Zuni *lhelo* (take a nap); African *lok* (gentle) and Zuni *lika* (gentle); African *eri* (go) and Zuni *ela* (move); and African *hru* (pleasing) and Zuni *elu* (pleasing).
6. *Nasal sonants* ("nose humming").
    a. African m equals Zuni m, as in African *mou* (cat) and Zuni *musa* (cat).

Copper ingot, 99% copper, from Hagia Triada in Crete, Middle

Cyprus

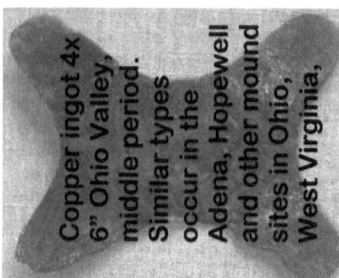

Copper ingot 4x 6" Ohio Valley, middle period. Similar types occur in the Adena, Hopewell and other mound sites in Ohio, West Virginia.

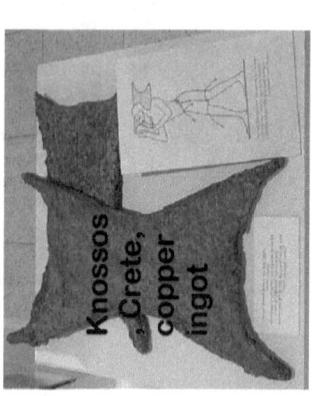

Knossos, Crete, copper ingot

American mound sites have yielded considerable numbers of copper tablets shaped like the hide of an animal; the function of these was unknown, and they were named "reels." However, in 1896 in Cyprus, and subsequently in many Mediterranean excavations, corresponding Bronze Age copper objects, recognized now as ingots used as international Bronze Age currency, have been found. The American

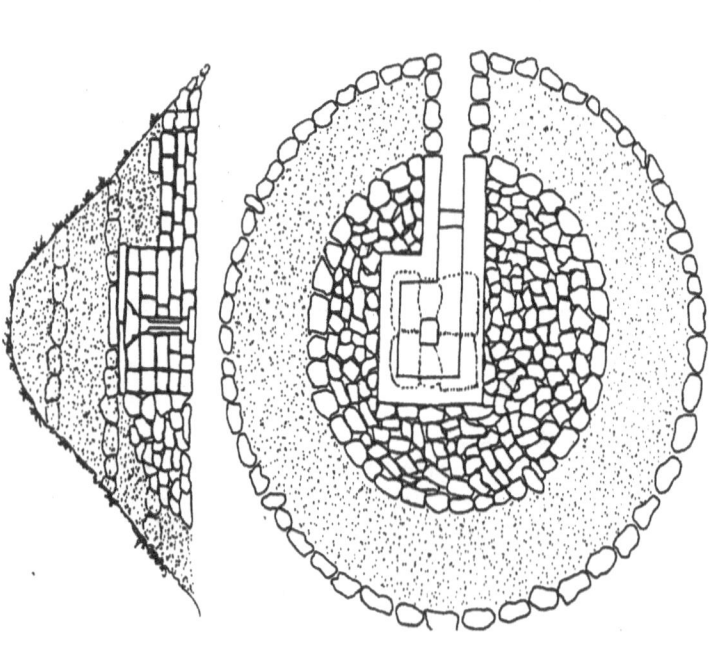

During the Bronze Age Iberian chiefs and kings were buried in mounds of varying size, similar to this example from Portugal, the body being placed in a stone-lined chamber about 60 feet deep beneath the summit of the mound or tumulus. The corresponding mounds of eastern and middle United States had timber chambers rather than stone, but they contain similar archeological remains to those found in

Who was Found in da Mounds?

Pyramid of the Sun, Teotihuacán, as it appears today.

the surface of the uppermost platform. Child sacrifices had been placed at the corners of each level. They crumbled to dust upon exposure to the air. The pyramid was surrounded with a great platform nineteen feet high and one hundred twenty-six feet wide. Beautifully decorated houses lay nearby.

Just as Batres was nearing the end of his work, political unrest caused him to abandon Teotihuacán forever. By that time, he estimated he had removed between twelve and twenty feet of earth from the outer surface of the pyramid. Batres's version of the Pyramid of the Sun was 203 feet high and 745 by 684 feet at the base. His many enemies were appalled at the damage. They accused him of having stripped off the outer layers of the pyramid as if it were an onion and of having mangled it beyond repair. When President Diaz was abruptly deposed in 1910, Batres fell from grace, leaving the field open to better-qualified archaeologists.

Batres's successor, a man of very different caliber, had been specially trained at Columbia University under the great an-

The Street of the Dead at Teotihuacán, viewed from the top of the Pyramid of the Moon. The Pyramid of the Sun is the large structure on the left.

tryside. Small villages of thatched huts dotted the distant landscape. From the heady elevation of the pyramid, Teotihuacán was truly a wonderful sight.

Any traveler to Teotihuacán first made a beeline for the market. There were several markets in the city, but the largest flourished in a huge open compound off the Street of the Dead, opposite the Temple of Quetzalcoatl. The markets supplied the needs of the entire city, a teeming urban population estimated to have once been as high as 100,000 people. While the priests and craftsworkers lived in dwellings built around small courtyards, the less privileged dwelt in large compounds of rooms connected by narrow alleyways and patios. Most of these people were urban dwellers who bought their staple diet of maize, squashes, and beans in the market. There were few farmers within the confines of Teotihuacán itself, but we know that many rural villages flourished nearby. Most of them were compact and expertly planned settlements whose

Who was Found in da Mounds?

The bones of *Negroid* GIANTS.

Articles by Albinos rarely admit these GIANTS are Negroid. Twould be incorrect to call them AFRICOID. Because nappy-spiral-haired BLAK people are INDIGENOUS to north & south AMERICA, as well as Afraka. Blak people are indigenous to the entire planet. ....and the very Cosmos. We are from Everywhere. The very word INDIGENOUS is INDI (Blak)+ GEN (beGINning); the Source (GENe, beGINning) is Blak. Even the word HUMAN is HUE (color!) Man. Dr. Richard King wrote: "The All Black neuromelanin nerve tract of the [Human] brain is profound proof that the human race is a Black race, with many variations of Black, from Black-Black to White-Black, all internally rooted in a vast sea of Brain Blackness."

Back to them mounds.
Following are clips from internet articles :

Giants in the Pyramids of America
Skeletons of tall, "giants," with distinctly African features have been found in many of these "Mound -[s]" which Africa-Americans including the Washitaw Nation regard as sacred sites and pyramids. Many of these structures are over three thousand years old and have been dated based on carbon-dating of artefacts found in them, although some have been dated to being settled about 900 A.D.

Pedro de Castaneda, who accompanied Coronado, wrote of the Cocopa Indian tribe that they were giants who could carry logs that six of the Spaniards could not budge. Archeological discoveries are numerous as well. In 1833 soldiers digging at Lompock Rancho, California, discovered a male skeleton 12 feet tall. The skeleton was surrounded

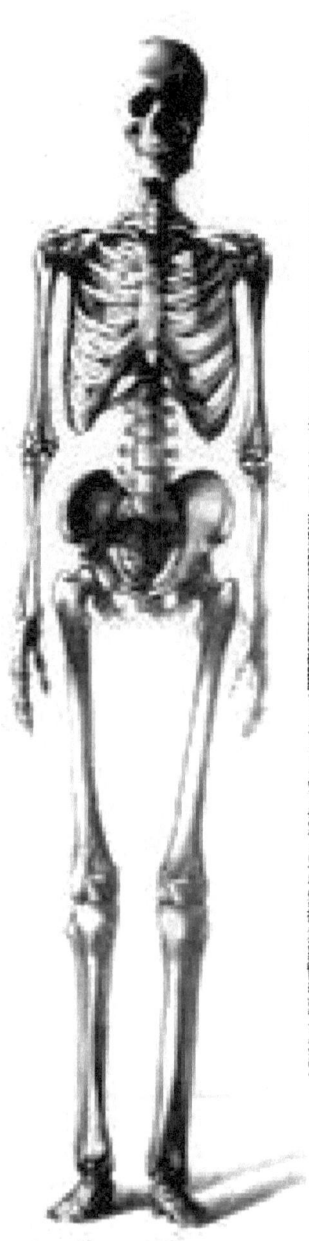

In his book, *The Natural and Aboriginal History of Tennessee*, author John Haywood describes "very large" bones in stone graves found in Williamson County, Tennessee, in 1821. In White County, Tennessee, an "ancient fortification" contained skeletons of gigantic stature averaging at least 7 feet in length.

Giant skeletons were found in the mid-1800s near Rutland and Rodman, New York. J.N. DeHart, M.D. found vertebrae "larger than those of the present type" in Wisconsin mounds in 1876. W.H.R. Lykins uncovered skull bones "of great size and thickness" in mounds of Kansas City area in 1877.

History of Morrow County and Ohio, 1880:
In 1829, when the hotel was built in Chesterville, a mound near by was made to furnish the material for the brick. In digging it away, a large human skeleton was found, but no measurements were made. It is related that the jaw-bone [sic] was found to fit easily over that of a citizen of the village, who was remarkable for his large jaw. The local physicians examined the cranium and found it proportionately large, with more teeth than the white race of today. The skeleton was taken to Mansfield, and has been lost sight of entirely.

A History of Ashtabula County, Ohio, 1878:
The graves were, distinguished by slight depressions in the surface of the earth, disposed in straight rows, which, with intervening spaces or valleys, covered the entire area. The number of these graves has been estimated to be between two and three thousand. Aaron Wright, Esq., in 1800, made a careful examination of these depressions, and found them invariably to contain human bones blackened with time, which upon exposure to the air soon crumbled to dust. Some of these bones were of unusual size, and evidently belonged to a race allied to giants. Skulls were taken from these mounds, the cavities of which were of sufficient capacity to admit the head of an ordinary man, and jaw-bones [sic] that might be fitted over the face with equal facility. The bones of the upper and lower extremities were of corresponding size.

Barverville, Indianna 1879:
A 9-foot, 8-inch skeleton was excavated from a nearby mound. (Indianapolis News, Nov. 10, 1975)

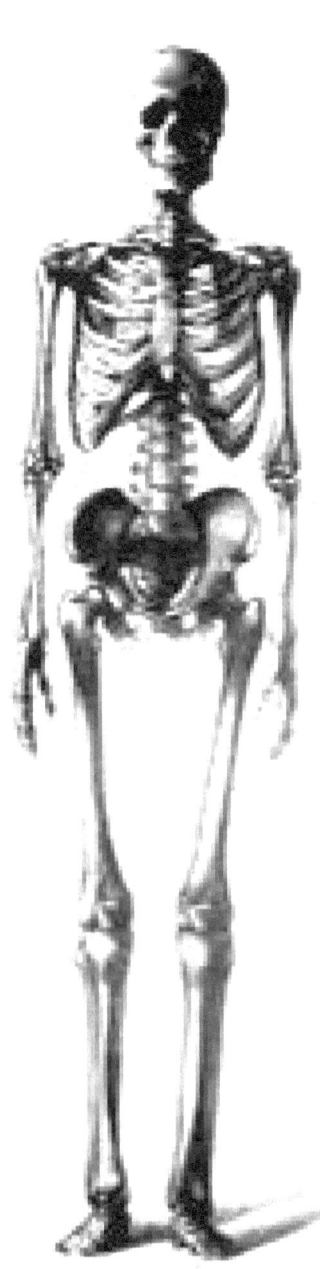

Zanesville, Ohio:
"...An enormous skeleton found in a mound in a clay coffin with a sandstone slab containing Hieroglyphics."
(American Antiquarian, v. 3, 1880)

Warren, Minnesota, 1883:
10 skeletons of both sexes and gigantic size were taken from a mound. (St. Paul Pioneer Press, May 23, 1883)

Kanawha County, West Virginia, 1884:
"A skeleton '7 feet 6 inches long, and 19 inches across the chest,' was removed from a massive stone structure that was likened to a temple chamber within a mound." (American Antiquarian, v. 6, 1884)

Minnesota, 1888:
"Discovered remains of 7 skeletons, 'seven to eight feet tall.' " (St. Paul Pioneer Press, June 29, 1888)

Toledo, Ohio 1895:
A mound near Toledo, Ohio held 20 skeletons, seated and facing East, with jaws and teeth twice as large as those of present day people; and beside each was a large bowl with "curiously wrought Hieroglyphical figures." (Chicago Record, Oct. 24, 1895 –cited by Ton G. Dobbins, NEARA Journal, v. 13, Fall 1978)

From Historical Text:
when the Whites arrived, Western New York was littered with the works of earlier people. Stone walls, graded roads, and fortifications were reported, though most commonly these markers were earthen mounds or enclosures. The Native Americans seldom had any tradition about the people who had put them in place. Most of us now believe that the influence of the Mississippian (Mound-Builder) culture was behind them. The settlement and the plow have been lethal to most of these fragile works, and even the old mound-fanatic E. G. Squier confessed ruefully in 1849 that the Western Door held little any more worth looking at. As these works were destroyed in the last century a stablefull of curiosities seems to have come out.

"T. Apoleon Cheney notes (in Illustrations of the Ancient Monuments of Western New York) that a twelve-foot high elliptical mound above Cattaraugus County's Conewango Valley held eight big skeletons. Most crumbled, but a thigh bone was found to be 28" long. Exquisite stone points, enamelwork, and

THE
ANCIENT LANDMARK.

A. C. SMITH, Editor & Proprietor.

Devoted to Masonry, Literature, and the Arts.

The individual who is accounted worthy to wear the badge of a free and accepted Mason, will find a long path strewed on either hand with so many familiar admonitions to the constant practice of all those cardinal principles so congenial to the well being of society, that he must be frail indeed if he be not benefited by his connection with our Order.—ED. LANDMARK.

VOLUME THREE.

M. H. MARSH, . . PUBLISHER.
MT. CLEMENS, MICHIGAN.
1853 & 4.

From the Placerville (Cal.) Herald.
DISCOVERY OF AN ANCIENT AMERICAN PYRAMID.

Travelers upon the Colorado and its tributaries have long since spoken of the existence of ancient ruins in different localities, embraced by the great American desert, lying upon both, though principally upon the west bank of the Colorado, and between it and the California range of mountains. Even Baron Von Humboldt, during his researches upon the American continent, discovered unmistakable evidence of the existence, at some greatly remote period, of a race of people entirely unlike, and apparently superior to, those inhabiting the continent at the time of its discovery by Europeans.

These evidences are becoming every day more and more conclusive, as the energy, love of travel and novelty, of the American people lead them into earth's wildest fastnesses, and over its most forbidden, sterile and inhospitable waste. We remark, as above, on perusing an article from the pen of our San Bernardino correspondent, giving an account of an ancient pyramid, lately discovered upon the great desert of the Colorado by a party of adventurers—five in number, who attempted to cross the desert in a westerly direction from a point on the Colorado at least two hundred miles above its confluence with the Gila:

San Bernardino Valley, June 23.

There has been no little excitement here of late, among the antiquarians and the curious, arising from the discovery of an ancient pyramid upon the great Colorado desert, and which fixes the probability beyond all dispute of the possession and occupancy, at some greatly remote period of time, of the American continent by a race of people of whom all existing history is silent.

A party of men, five in number, had ascended the Colorado for nearly two hundred miles above the mouth of the Gila, there object being to discover, if possible, some large tributary from the west, by which they might make the passage of the desert, and enter California by a new, more direct and easier route, inasmuch as there are known to exist numerous small streams upon the eastern slope of the mountains; that are either lost in the sands of the desert or unite with the Colorado, through tributaries heretofore unknown. They represent the country on one side of the Colorado as almost totally barren of every vegetable product, and so level and monotonous that any object sufficient to arrest the attention possesses more or less of curiosity and interest; and it was this that led to the discovery and examination of this hitherto unknown relic of a forgotten age.

An object appeared upon the plain to the west, having so much the appearance of a work of art, from the regularity of its outline, and its isolated position, that the party determined upon visiting it. Passing over an almost barren sand plain, a distance of nearly five miles, they reached the base of one of the most wonderful objects, considering its location (it being the very home of desolation) that the mind can scarcely conceive of; nothing less than an immense stone pyramid, composed of layers or courses of from eighteen inches to nearly three feet in thickness, and from five to eight feet in length. It has a level top of more than fifty feet square, though it is evident that it was once completed; but that some great convulsion of nature has displaced its entire top, as it evidently now lies a huge and broken mass upon one of its sides, though nearly covered by the sands.

This pyramid differs, in some respects, from the Egyptian pyramid. It is, or was more slender or pointed, and while those of Egypt are composed of steps or layers, receding as they rise, the American pyramid was, undoubtedly, a more finished structure. The outer surface of the blocks was evidently cut to an angle, that gave the structure, when new and complete, a smooth or regular surface from top to bot-

(1402-1413) which followed the defeat of his father by Tamerlane; he was thus the second founder of the Ottoman Empire.

During the interregnum, he eliminated his brothers one by one and restored a united Ottoman state in Western Anatolia and Thrace. After 1413 he abandoned his father's policy of forceful advance into Anatolia and concentrated on regaining the Ottoman possessions in the Balkans. He conquered most of Albania (1415), secured the vassalage of Wallachia in southern Romania (1416) and the Byzantine state (1417), raided across the Danube into Hungary, and capped the reconquest by restoring the Ottoman capital to Adrianople (Edirne). Mehmed inaugurated a policy of settling in the Balkans the restless and rebellious Turkoman tribes of Anatolia. This not only relieved Anatolia of the threat of nomadic insecurity, but also helped the Ottomans to reduce to obedience the mountainous and less accessible areas of the Balkans, which could not be conquered by the regular Ottoman army. Mehmed's efforts to raid and capture some of the Venetian-controlled islands of the Aegean Sea were largely turned back, and the small Ottoman navy was destroyed by the Venetian fleet in a naval battle in 1415.

While Mehmed largely avoided conquest in Anatolia, he did defeat a coalition formed against him by the principal Anatolian Turkish princes (1418), suppressed the widespread revolts of an Anatolian mystic order led by Sheik Bedruddin, and in general ruled firmly in the areas under his dominion. The solid foundation of empire which he established enabled his successors to complete the reconquest of the Ottoman realm.

Mehmed I died in 1421 and was succeeded by his son Murad II.

Mehmed II (1432-1481), who reigned from 1444 to 1446 and then from 1451 to 1481, was son of Murad II and the seventh sultan of the Ottoman Empire. He is called Fatih, "the Conqueror," by the Turks.

Mehmed II effected the final destruction of the Byzantine Empire by capturing Istanbul in 1453. Three years later he completed the reconquest of the empire of Bayazid I by capturing Belgrade. He then took advantage of the administrative and military consolidation achieved by his predecessors, Mehmed I and Murad II, to move forcefully into Anatolia and conquer the previously independent Turkish principalities and the last Byzantine colony at Trebizond (1461).

These conquests brought the Ottoman Empire into conflict with strong states in both West and East. In Europe, Hungary contested the Ottoman advance beyond the Danube and Venice fought the Ottomans in Greece, Albania, and the Aegean Sea. In the East, the Ak Koyunlu ("White Sheep") Empire of the famous Uzun Hasan, which had succeeded the Timurid Empire in Iran, fought against Mehmed in Eastern Anatolia. And to the southeast, Mehmed's conquests as far as the Euphrates River brought him to the borders of the Mameluke Empire of Egypt and Syria. After 1460 Venice, Hungarym and the Ak Koyunlu, inspired by the appeals fo the Pope, united against Ottomans, Bayazid I had succumbed to similar foreign enemies one by one and made secure and definitive the Ottoman Empire between the Danube and the Euphrates.

SULTAN MEHMED II, the conqueror of Constantinople.

Mehmed II succeeded where Bayazid I failed because Mehmed inherited and continued the work of his predecessors of consolidating the Ottoman rule in conquered territories before attempting new conquests. He tried to relieve the economic and social stresses caused by the long period of war and sudden acquisition of vast new territories and peoples, thus making sure that his empire would not fall apart under foreign pressure. This work was carried forward under his son and successor, Bayazid II.

Mehmed II was also the first Ottoman Sultan to conquer successfully the political power of the old Turkish aristocracy in the Ottoman ruling class. He did this by building up the Devshirme class of non-Muslims converted to Islam and rewarded for their services by salaries paid by the Sultan, rather than by the Timar fief which had made the Turkish aristocracy financially independent. Mehmed II assured the Devshirme class of power sufficient to match that of the new Janizary salaried infantry corps, which was created to make use of the new cannos and rifles then being introduced for the first time.. He successfully balanced the power of the Turkish aristocracy against that of the Devshirme and therefore was able to use both for his own purposes.

Mehmed III (1566-1603), who reigned from 1595 to 1603,was a son of Murad III and the 13th Sultan of the Ottoman Empire. Mehmed III ruled at a time when the power of the palace women in the government reached its peak and the previous Ottoman decline was transformed into actual integration.

Mehmed was the last Ottoman sultan to serve as a provincial administrator before his accession. Subsequently, the sons of the of the ruling sultan were isolated in the palace without principle education or training. Their accession was secured entirely by their mothers rather than as a result of experience or ability , and they were completely under the influence of the harem. Mehmed III was the last Ottoman sultan to lead personally the Ottoman army.

During his reign there occurred the first of a series of disastrous defeats inflicted on the Ottoman army in East and West. In Europe, the Hapsburg army routed the Ottomans in several critical battles, although decisive territorial losses were temporarily averted by great Ottoman victories over the Hapsburgs at the Battle of Hach Ova in Northern Hungary (1596) All over Anatolia, Turkish national revolts broke out against the Devshirme and harem misrule in Istanbul. Although the Istanbul government was still able to summon sufficient military force to suppress most of them, these revolts deprived the central government of the bulk of its revenues from Anatolia and the Arab provinces and also greatly hindered the operations of the Ottoman army in the East. A new Iranian ruler Abbas I, was able to take advantage of this to drive the Ottoman forces out of Azerbaidzhan and most of the Caucusus.

Mehmed III died in 1603 and was succeeded by his heir, Ahmed I.

Mehmed IV (1641-1693) who reigned from 1648 to 1693 was a son of Sultan Ibrahim and the 19th sultan of the Ottoman Empire. His reign marked the culmination of the Quran.

MOORS AND THE AMERICAN REVOLUTION

We are often told that the first man to die for the American Revolution was a black man by the name of Crispus Attucks, one of the many Black(a)Moors who were involved with the War of Independence. The mention of Attucks is a feeble attempt to hide the truth:

1. The Moors were at, if not THE very foundation and cornerstone of the creation of the United States republic.
2. The Constitution for the United States of America was adopted from the Moors.
3. The land was ceded to their said government by the Moors.
4. At least half the signatories to the Declaration of Independence were Moors.
5. The architect who designed their capitol city, Washington, D.C. was designed by a Moor.

At every phase of America's development you find Moors (black people). The following images will help to give a visual validation and comprehension of the author's words. The book *Black Courage*, written by the Daughters of the American Revolution— one group tasked as gatekeepers through the annals of Moorish American history. This publication show the facts about Moors/blacks involved in every aspect of the America's military, but as you know, most recounting of this period in history fail to mention these contributions.

When and if these colonial invaders decide to tell the whole truth, and nothing but the truth, the world will come to acknowledge the land known as America as "dark" a continent as they consider Africa.

Crispus Attucks

IN BOSTON, Massachusetts on the evening of March 5, 1770, British soldiers fired their muskets at point-blank range into a crowd of protesters, led by "a stout man with a long stick." The "stout man," later identified by an eyewitness as "the molatto (sic)," Crispus Attucks, was the first to fall, "killed on the spot with two balls entering his breast." This event, later known as the Boston Massacre, was the culmination of the resentment and outrage felt by the citizens of Boston as a result of soldiers being quartered on their property by order of the King, to enforce laws passed in England without their consent. The most despised of these laws was The Stamp Act, (1765) and later, the tax on tea, (1773) which resulted in the "Boston Tea Party."

John Adams, later the second president of the United States, stated at the trial of the soldiers for the deaths of Attucks and the four others, Samuel Gray, Samuel Maverick, James Caldwell and Patrick Carr, that "This Attucks appeared to have undertaken to be the hero of the night; and to lead the army . . . to form them in the first place in Dock Square, and march them up King Street (now State Street) with their clubs . . ." The five men killed that night were buried together in a common grave, and Crispus Attucks, who, with his cordwood stick had raised his arm against the soldiers of King George III, became the first martyr of the American Revolution.

Crispus Attucks

IN BOSTON, Massachusetts on the evening of March 5, 1770, British soldiers fired their muskets at point-blank range into a crowd of protesters, led by "a stout man with a long stick." The "stout man," later identified by an eyewitness as "the molatto (sic)," Crispus Attucks, was the first to fall, "killed on the spot with two balls entering his breast." This event, later known as the Boston Massacre, was the culmination of the resentment and outrage felt by the citizens of Boston as a result of soldiers being quartered on their property by order of the King, to enforce laws passed in England without their consent. The most despised of these laws was The Stamp Act, (1765) and later, the tax on tea, (1773) which resulted in the "Boston Tea Party."

John Adams, later the second president of the United States, stated at the trial of the soldiers for the deaths of Attucks and the four others, Samuel Gray, Samuel Maverick, James Caldwell and Patrick Carr, that "This Attucks appeared to have undertaken to be the hero of the night; and to lead the army . . . to form them in the first place in Dock Square, and march them up King Street (now State Street) with their clubs . . ." The five men killed that night were buried together in a common grave, and Crispus Attucks, who, with his cordwood stick had raised his arm against the soldiers of King George III, became the first-martyr of the American Revolution.

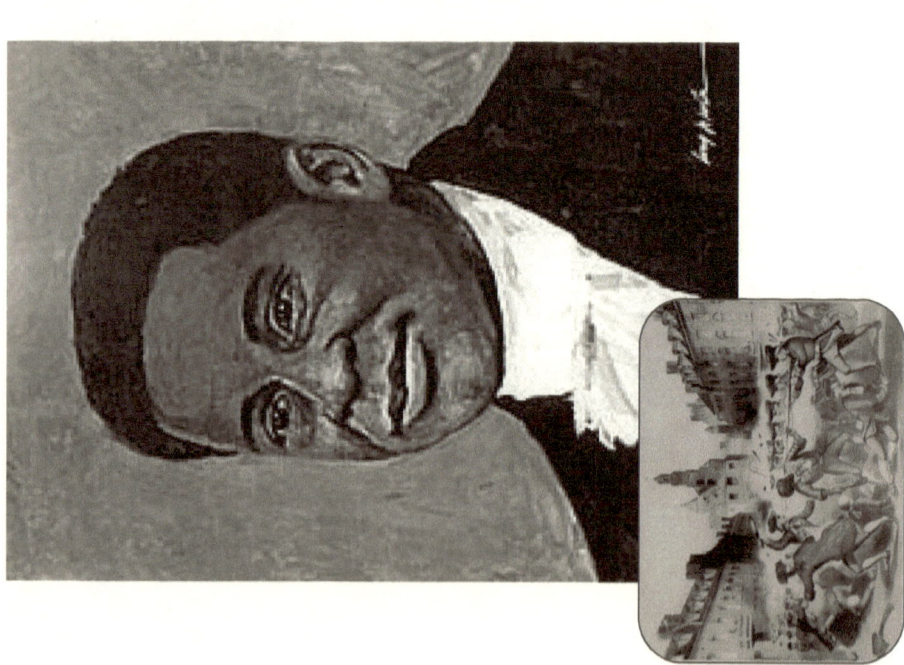

BLACK COURAGE

1775–1783

Documentation Of Black Participation In The American Revolution

Robert Ewell Greene

PUBLISHED BY
NATIONAL SOCIETY
OF THE
DAUGHTERS OF THE AMERICAN REVOLUTION
WASHINGTON: 1984

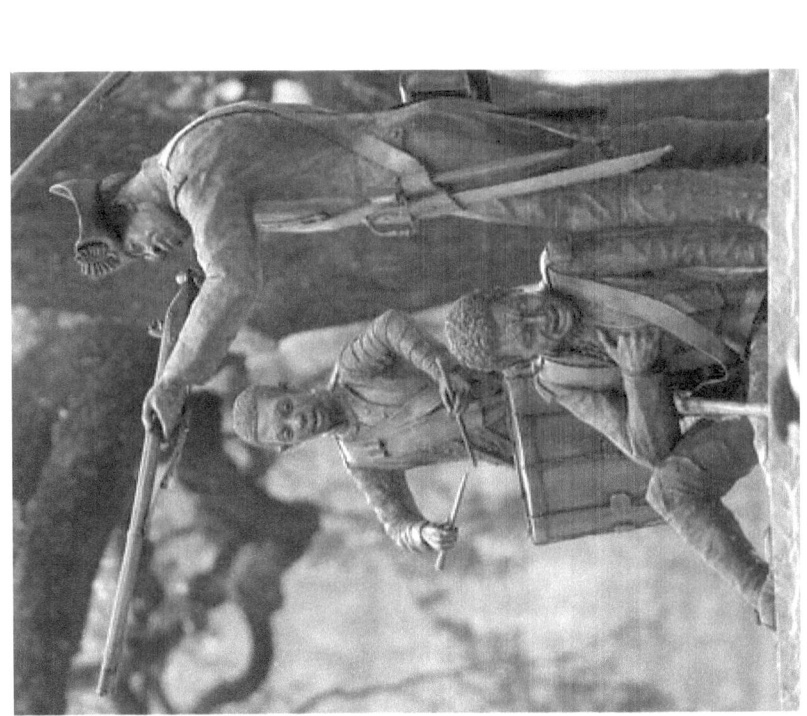

Colonists armed about 5,000 blacks for battle against the "Tories," or royalists, during the American Revolution. Meanwhile, British forces enlisted Native Americans who wanted colonists off their hunting and farming lands.

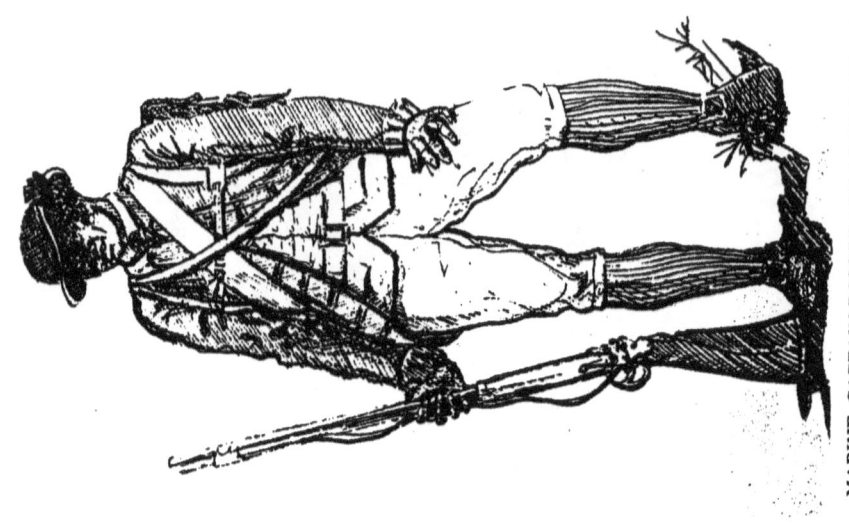

MARINE, CAPTAIN ROBERT MULLAN'S COMPANY

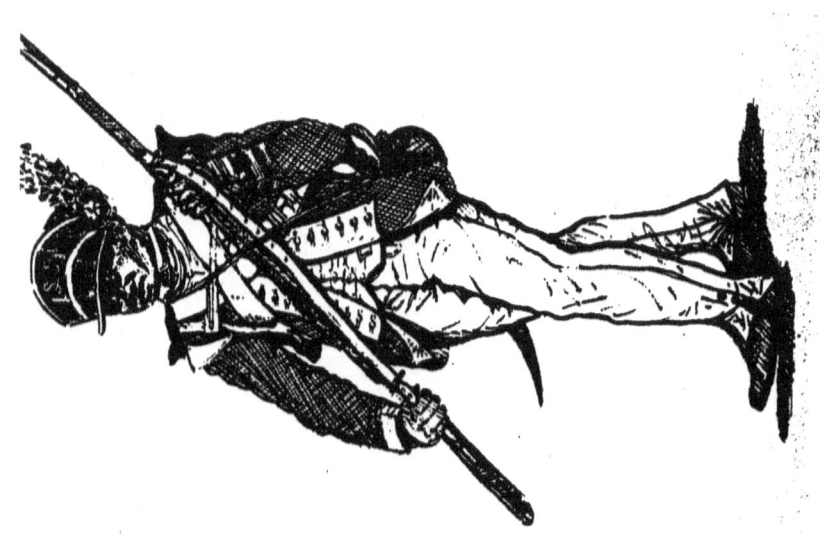

PRIVATE, FOURTH MASSACHUSETTS REGIMENT, 1781–1782

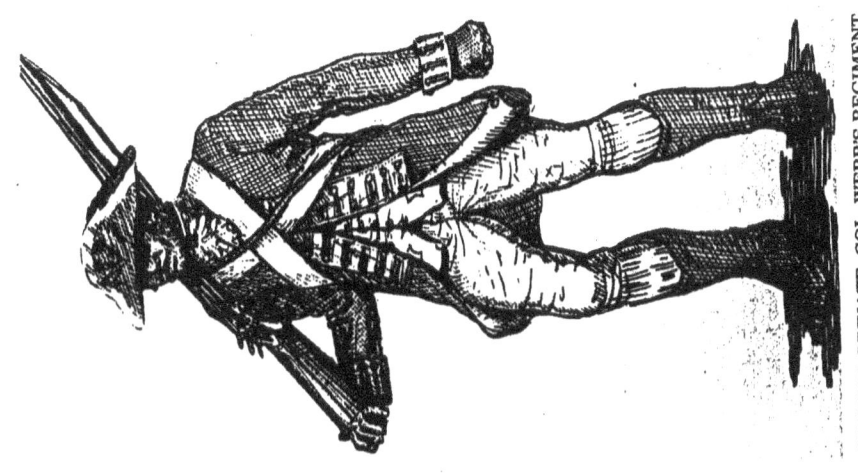

SOLDIER, PRIVATE, COL. WEBB'S REGIMENT, CONTINENTAL LINE

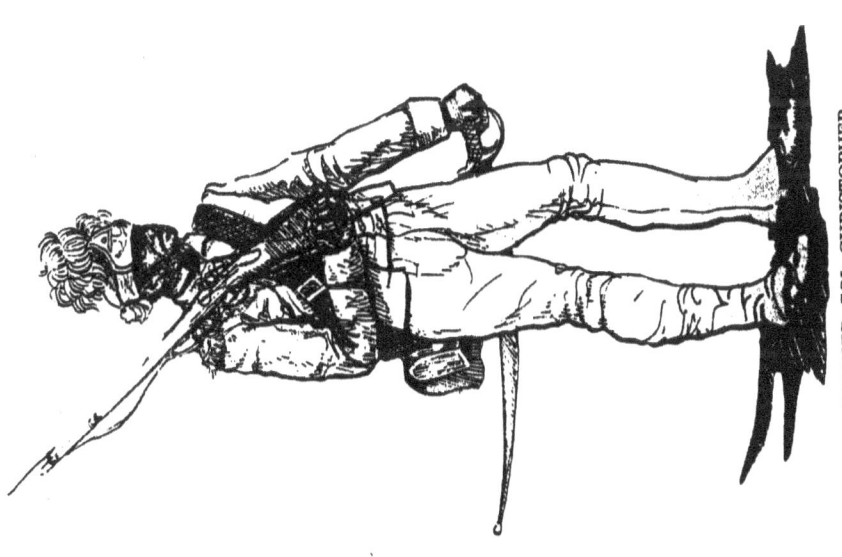

SOLDIER, COL. CHRISTOPHER GREENE'S BLACK RHODE ISLAND REGIMENT

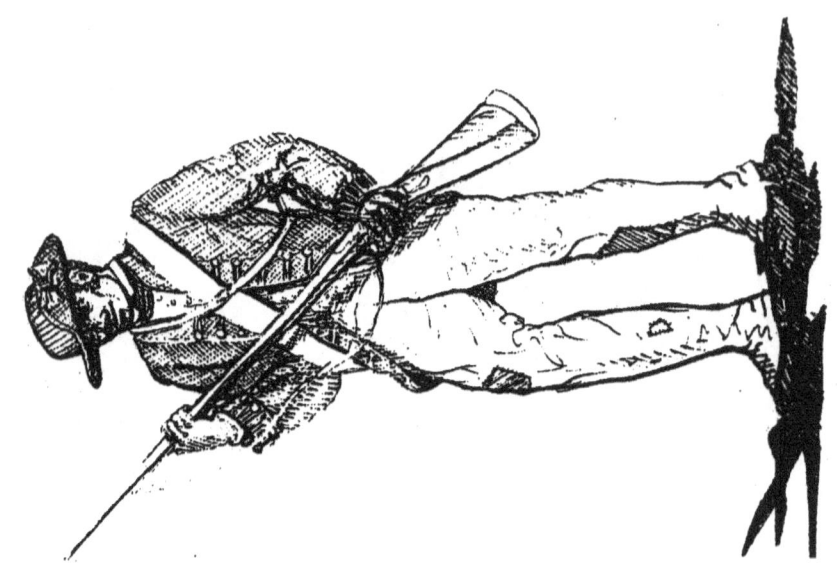

SOLDIER, PRIVATE, SECOND VIRGINIA REGIMENT

SOLDIER, MARYLAND BATTALION OF FLYING CAMP

PETER SALEM
American Revolution

During the American Revolution many Blacks fought with the hope, and in some cases promises, of being free men when the war ended. However, many of their dreams of freedom were cut short when the Continental Congress decided to pass a law forbidding slaves to fight, for fear that arming the slaves could lead to a revolt. Under this decision, Peter Salem, a slave, would have been forced to leave the Continental Army. However, his owners, the Belknaps of Framingham, granted Salem his freedom thereby making him eligible for military services because free men were able to serve. During the Battle of Bunker Hill, fought on June 17, 1775, Salem, obeying the orders not to fire "until you see the whites of their eyes" is credited with the shot that killed British Major Pitcairn, who foolishly leapt on the wall to claim victory. Salem also fought at Concord and Saratoga. In memory of Peter Salem, who died on this day in 1816, the Sons of the American Revolution of Framingham, Massachusetts erected a memorial.

Oliver Cromwell (May 24, 1752 – January 1853) was an African-American soldier, who served in the American Revolutionary War. He was born a free black in Black Horse (now the Columbus section of Mansfield Township, Burlington County, New Jersey), and was raised as a farmer.

Private Cromwell served in several companies of the 2nd New Jersey Regiment between 1777 and 1783, seeing action at the battles of Trenton (1776), Princeton (1777), Brandywine (1777), Monmouth (1778), and at the final siege of Yorktown (1781).

After Yorktown, Cromwell left the army. Commander-in-Chief George Washington personally signed Cromwell's discharge papers and also designed the Badge of Military Merit, which he awarded to Cromwell.

Some years after retirement, Cromwell applied for a veteran's pension. Although he was unable to read or write, local lawyers, judges and politicians came to his aid, and he was granted a pension of $96 a year. He purchased a 100-acre farm outside Burlington, fathered 14 children, then spent his later years at his home at 114 East Union Street in Burlington. Cromwell is depicted in the famous *Washington Crossing the Delaware* portrait.

Benjamin Banneker was born a freeman on November 9, 1731, to Mary and Robert Bannaky in an area of Baltimore County, Maryland, between Oella and Ellicott City. Much of Benjamin's early life was greatly influenced by the strength and determination of his grandmother, Molly Walsh. She taught Benjamin how to read from the only book available, the Bible. When he became a proficient reader, Benjamin was sent to a Quaker school. Reportedly it was his Quaker schoolmaster who changed Benjamin's last name from Bannaky to Banneker.

Benjamin Banneker enjoyed the outdoors. He also enjoyed playing the flute and violin when not working on his parents' farm. With his strong mathematical skills and interest in learning, Banneker grew up to be an excellent farmer. One day at the store, Banneker met a man who showed him a pocket watch. He was so consumed by the concept of time that he borrowed the watch, took it apart very carefully, and made notes as he studied each piece. Using a pocketknife, he carved each gear out of wood and put the wooden gears together, creating the first striking clock made completely out of wood. Banneker was only 22 years old at the time and was admired by many.

Andrew Ellicott, commissioned as a surveyor to help construct the boundaries of what is now Washington, D.C., was charged with the responsibility of hiring competent assistants. His cousin George was unavailable and suggested that he ask Benjamin Banneker to assist him. Banneker was 60 years old at the time, but he was excited by the opportunity and agreed to help. The winter of 1791, Banneker worked into the early hours of the morning making all the necessary calculations. The task was finally completed in April, and Banneker returned to his farm, where he finished the astronomical predictions for his 1792 almanac.

During the colonial period, an almanac was very important, and most families owned one. Banneker spent several months making the calculations for his first almanac. Using his keen mathematical sense, Banneker predicted eclipses and computed detailed information about the rising and setting of the sun. Yet he had difficulty getting his almanac published, so he wrote a letter to Thomas Jefferson, who was then the Secretary of State. Within ten days Jefferson had replied to Banneker and complimented his almanac, which would be the first of six, was printed soon after this recognition.

THE FIRST UNITED STATES OF AMERICA AND ITS FIRST CONSTITUTION

Most Americans are not familiar with the true history of America, but rather with his-story. FACT: The Constitution of the United States existed long before the so-called founding fathers plagiarized it and claimed it as their own. The one clue they left of this fact is contained the first paragraph of this greatest document; "We the People **adopt** this Constitution..."

THE FIRST UNITED IROQUIOS NATIONS OF AMERICA

COMMONLY KNOWN AS THE SIX NATIONS
1. The Mohawk
2. The Seneca
3. The Cayuga
4. The Oneida
5. The Onodaga
6. The Adodarhoh

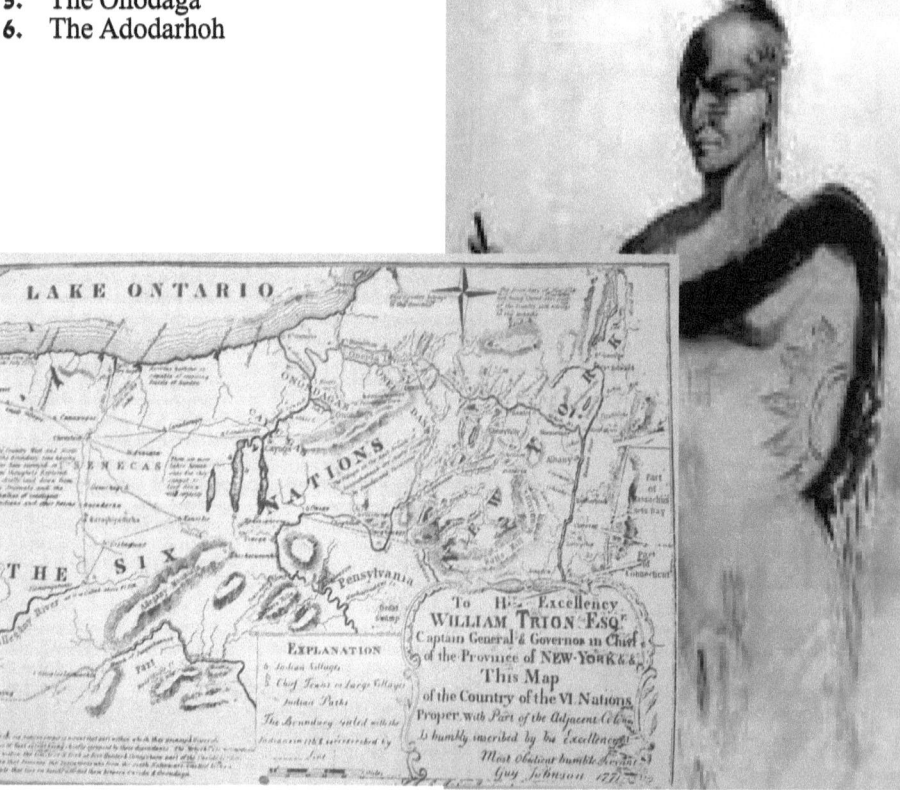

Constitution of the Iroquois Nations:

THE GREAT BINDING LAW, GAYANASHAGOWA

1. I am Dekanawidah and with the Five Nations' Confederate Lords I plant the Tree of Great Peace. I plant it in your territory, Adodarhoh, and the Onondaga Nation, in the territory of you who are Firekeepers.

I name the tree the Tree of the Great Long Leaves. Under the shade of this Tree of the Great Peace we spread the soft white feathery down of the globe thistle as seats for you, Adodarhoh, and your cousin Lords.

We place you upon those seats, spread soft with the feathery down of the globe thistle, there beneath the shade of the spreading branches of the Tree of Peace. There shall you sit and watch the Council Fire of the Confederacy of the Five Nations, and all the affairs of the Five Nations shall be transacted at this place before you, Adodarhoh, and your cousin Lords, by the Confederate Lords of the Five Nations.

2. Roots have spread out from the Tree of the Great Peace, one to the north, one to the east, one to the south and one to the west. The name of these roots is The Great White Roots and their nature is Peace and Strength.

If any man or any nation outside the Five Nations shall obey the laws of the Great Peace and make known their disposition to the Lords of the Confederacy, they may trace the Roots to the Tree and if their minds are clean and they are obedient and promise to obey the wishes of the Confederate Council, they shall be welcomed to take shelter beneath the Tree of the Long Leaves.

We place at the top of the Tree of the Long Leaves an Eagle who is able to see afar. If he sees in the distance any evil approaching or any danger threatening he will at once warn the people of the Confederacy.

3. To you Adodarhoh, the Onondaga cousin Lords, I and the other Confederate Lords have entrusted the caretaking and the watching of the Five Nations Council Fire.

When there is any business to be transacted and the Confederate Council is not in session, a messenger shall be dispatched either to Adodarhoh, Hononwirehtonh or Skanawatih, Fire Keepers, or to their War Chiefs with a full statement of the case desired to be considered. Then shall Adodarhoh call his cousin (associate) Lords together and consider whether or not the case is of sufficient importance to demand the attention of the Confederate Council. If so, Adodarhoh shall dispatch messengers to summon all the Confederate Lords to assemble beneath the Tree of the Long Leaves.

When the Lords are assembled the Council Fire shall be kindled, but not with chestnut wood, and Adodarhoh shall formally open the Council.

Then shall Adodarhoh and his cousin Lords, the Fire Keepers, announce the subject for discussion.

The Smoke of the Confederate Council Fire shall ever ascend and pierce the sky so that other nations

Original paintings of Black Mohawk Indians in Moorish garb

5. The Council of the Mohawk shall be divided into three parties as follows: Tekarihoken, Ayonhwhathah and Shadekariwade are the first party; Sharenhowaneh, Deyoenhegwenh and Oghrenghrehgowah are the second party, and Dehennakrineh, Aghstawenserenthah and Shoskoharowaneh are the third party. The third party is to listen only to the discussion of the first and second parties and if an error is made or the proceeding is irregular they are to call attention to it, and when the case is right and properly decided by the two parties they shall confirm the decision of the two parties and refer the case to the Seneca Lords for their decision. When the Seneca Lords have decided in accord with the Mohawk Lords, the case or question shall be referred to the Cayuga and Oneida Lords on the opposite side of the house.

6. I, Dekanawidah, appoint the Mohawk Lords the heads and the leaders of the Five Nations Confederacy. The Mohawk Lords are the foundation of the Great Peace and it shall, therefore, be against the Great Binding Law to pass measures in the Confederate Council after the Mohawk Lords have protested against them.

No council of the Confederate Lords shall be legal unless all the Mohawk Lords are present.

Original paintings of Black Mohawk Indians in Moorish garb

Much of the terminology that the conquerors in the Spanish Borderlands used during this initial period was drawn from the religious crusades that the Christian kingdoms of the Iberian Peninsula waged against the forces of Islam during the Reconquest (711–1492). Explaining how the habits of warfare forged over centuries died slowly, Francisco López de Gómara, one of the chroniclers of Mexico's conquest, wrote in 1523 that since the Christians had long fought infidels, "the conquest of the Indies began when that of the Moors was over." Thus, despite the fact that there were few, if any, Moors in the Spanish Borderlands, it was not uncommon for the colonists there to refer to the Indians as Moors. The Indians were described as carrying "Moorish bows" (bows and arrows). They were accused of worshiping the devil in "mosques" (ceremonial chambers). And according to one Santa Fe resident, Joseph de Armijo, who suffered from insomnia, his sleeplessness in 1749 was due to a fear that "the Moors might attack unexpectedly."

43

DIGGING FOR THE RED ROOTS

Mahir Abdal-Razzaaq El

I am a Muslim from Cherokee Blackfoot American-Indian community. I am also known as Eagle Sun Walker and serve as a Pipe Carrier Warrior for the Northeastern Band of Cherokee Indians in New York City. There are other Muslims in our group.

Many people are not aware of the Native American contact with Islam that began more than one thousand years ago by some of the early Muslim travelers who visited us. Some of them lived among our people. Most Muslims and non-Muslims are not aware of this fact, and have never seen it mentioned in any of the history books. Many documents, treaties, legislation and resolutions, passed between 1600s and 1800s, show that Muslims were in fact here and were very active in their communities.

The *Peace and Friendship Treaty*, signed on the Delaware River in the year 1787, bears the signatures of Abdel-Khak and Muhammad Ibn Abdullah. This treaty details our continued right to exist as a community in the areas of commerce, maritime shipping, and our form of government which at that time was in accordance with Islam.

According to a federal court case from the *Continental Congress*, we help put the breath of life into the newly framed constitution. All of the documents are presently in the *National Archives* as well as the *Library of Congress*. If you have access to records in the state of South Carolina, read the *Moors Sundry Act of 1790*. [The Moors].

In a future article, Insha'Allah, I will go into more details about the various tribes, their languages, and the influence of Arabic, Persian, and Hebrew words on some of their languages. Almost all of the tribes vocabulary includes the word Allah (SWT). The traditional dress code for Indian women includes the *kimah* and long dresses. For men, the standard fare is turbans and long tops that come down to the knees. If you read any of the old books on Cherokee clothing up until 1832, you will see the men wearing turbans and the women wearing long head coverings. The last Cherokee's chief (1866) had a Muslim name *Ramadhan Ibn Wati*.

Cities across the United States and Canada bear names that are of Indian and Islamic derivation. Have you ever wondered what the name Tallahassee means? It means 'He, Allah, will deliver you sometime in the future.' In Cherokee, we refer to ourselves as Ani Getowagi or 'I am a township person.' [More on cities and descendents of Muslims among American-Indians].

> Allah: Allah is the Arabic word for The One and Only God, The Creator and Sustainer of the universe. It is used by the Arab Christians and Jews for the God (Eloh-im in Hebrew). The word Allah does not have a plural or gender. Allah does not have any associate or partner, and He does not beget nor was He begotten. SWT is an abbreviation of Arabic words that mean 'Glory Be To Him.'

Moulay al-Rashid (1631-1672) Sultan of Morocco 1666-1672, founder of the Alaouite Dynasty

MOULAY AL-RASHID (1631 – 1672) SULTAN OF MOROCCO (1666 – 1672) FOUNDER OF THE ALOUITE DYNASTY

Mulai al-Rashid (Arabic: مولاي الرشيد) was Sultan of Moroccofrom 1666 to 1672. He has been called the founder of the Alaouite Dynasty.

It was his father Moulay Ali Cherif who took power in Tafilalt around 1630. In 1635 al-Rashid's brother Ismail Ibn Sharif succeeded their still living father. After the death of their father, Mulai Mohammed brought Tafilalt, the Draa River valley and the Sahara region under Alouite power. However due to internal feuding war broke out between the brothers and Mohammed was killed by troops of al-Rashid in 1664.

With a small army al-Rashid ruled the east of Morocco. He was able to expand his power and seize Taza. In 1666 he marched into Fes and ended the rule of the zaouia of Dila, a Berber movement which ruled the northern part of Morocco. After subjugating the northern coastal areas of Morocco he also succeeded in capturing Marrakech in 1669. He occupied the Sus and the Little Atlas, which settled the Alaouite power over entire Morocco.

Who's the Moor???

Moroccan–American Treaty of Friendship Ratification dated July 18, 1787 by "Arthur St. Clair, our President, at the City of New York" - Image Courtesy of the Library of Congress

hides, both of which the Carthaginians re-exported to the eastern Mediterranean as supposed products of Gaul, the furs even reaching India. By the time the Romans conquered Spain and Carthage they had adequate alternate sources of these materials, and they took no interest in overseas shipping, having no merchant navy. The North American trade dwindled, the last phases presumably being operated by the maritime Celts of Brittany until their conquest by Caesar in 55 B.C. For 400 years after the Battle of Actium in 31 B.C. the Romans had no navy, since they had no rivals, and the memory of America apparently was lost. By 200 A.D. geographers believed that a voyage westward from Spain would lead to India and China, and this was the inheritance of Columbus.

12 + A Complete Armorial Achievement

A good example of an American armorial device, redrawn from the seal of the Ohio Company. The tilting helmet is correctly proportioned to the "heater"-shaped shield. The supporters are authentically costumed, easily identifiable as (dexter) a Plains Indian and (sinister) a Five Nations Indian. The beaver crest symbolizes industry; beaver was also a principal trade item. Three stags *statant reguardant* form a simple and easily recognizable arms. The motto states the Company aims — *Peace and Commerce*. (Note that the torse and mantling, as shown, are not part of the original seal. They have been added here only for the sake of completing the components of an achievement.)

The Ohio Company was formed in 1748 by London businessmen and Virginia planters led by Thomas Lee. Chartered in 1749 by George II, it was granted 500,000 acres west of the Appalachians and south of the Ohio, with the stipulation that 100 families be settled and a garrison maintained. Between 1749 and 1754 many storehouses were built and the surrounding country explored. The French and Indian War caused the settlers to flee in 1756 (the Five Nations were allies of the French) and an otherwise successful venture was abandoned.

After the Revolution another company — the Ohio Company of Associates — was formed to purchase the land between the Ohio and Lake Erie. Congress voted the sale of 1,500,000 acres to the company and granted additional plots free. The company was unable to pay in full, but a large tract was bought for nine cents an acre. The town of Marietta, Ohio was settled in 1788 and colonization and development proceeded at a rapid pace. This second company was headed by Rufus Putnam and Benjamin Tupper, both of whom were New Englanders.

An act authorizing the President of the United States to apply a further sum to the expense of the negotiations with the Dey and Regency of Algiers.

Be it enacted etc., That the President of the United States be, and be it hereby authorized to apply a sum not exceeding two hundred and fifty –nine dollars and three cents to the expenses which may have been incurred in any negotiations with the Dey and Regency of Algiers, beyond the sums heretofore appropriated; and that the said sum of two hundred and eighty thousand two hundred and fifty-nine dollars and three cents be, and the same is hereby, appropriated for that purpose.

SEC. 3 *And be it further enacted.* That the said several sums shall be paid and discharged out of any moneys arising from the revenues of the United States, beyond the appropriations heretofore charged thereupon to the end of the year one thousand seven hundred and ninety-seven.

Approved, March 3, 1797.

An act authorizing the President of the United States to apply a further sum to the expense of negotiations with the Dey and Regency of Algiers.

Be it enacted, &c., That the President of the United States be, and he is hereby, authorized to apply a sum not exceeding two hundred and eighty thousand two hundred and fifty-nine dollars and three cents to the expenses which may have been incurred in any negotiations with the Dey and Regency of Algiers, beyond the sums heretofore appropriated; and that the said sum of two hundred and eighty thousand two hundred and fifty-nine dollars and three cents be, and the same is hereby, appropriated for that purpose.

SEC. 2. *And be it further enacted,* That a further sum, not exceeding ninety-six thousand two hundred and forty-six dollars and sixty-three cents, be, and the same is hereby, appropriated for discharging the two first years' annuity to the Dey and Regency of Algiers, pursuant to treaty, in addition to the sum appropriated for that purpose by the act of the sixth of May, one thousand seven hundred and ninety-six.

SEC. 3. *And be it further enacted,* That the said several sums shall be paid and discharged out of any moneys arising from the revenues of the United States, beyond the appropriations heretofore charged thereupon, to the end of the year one thousand seven hundred and ninety-seven.

Approved, March 3, 1797.

seven hundred and ninety-five, the money arising under the revenue laws of the United States, which have been heretofore passed, not already appropriated to any other purpose, or so much thereof as may be necessary, be, and are hereby pledged and appropriated for the payment of the annuity stipulated in the said treaty, to be paid to the said Indian tribes ; that is to say, to the Wyandots, one thousand dollars; to the Delaware, one thousand dollars; to the Shawnees, one thousand dollars; to the Chippewas, one thousand dollars; to the Pattawatimas, one thousand dollars; to the Miamis, one thousand dollars; to the Eel-River, Wea, Kickapoo, Piankeshaw, and Kaskaskias tribes, each five hundred dollars; and to continue so pledged and appropriated so long as the said treaty shall be in force. And that a further sum of one thousand dollars out of the moneys aforesaid, be also appropriated to defray the cost of transportation, and other contingent charges which may arise from the payment of said annuity, according to the stipulations contained in the said treaty.

Approved, May 6, 1796

An Act making an appropriation for the defraying the expenses which may arise in carrying into effect the Treaty made between the United States and the Dey and Regency of Algiers.

Be it enactied etc. That, for the purpose of defraying the expenses of carrying into effect the Treaty made between the United States and the Dey and Regency of Algiers, the moneys arising under the revenue laws of the United States; which have been heretofore passed, not already appropriated to any other purpose, or so much thereof as may be necessary, to the amount of twenty-four thousand dollars per annum, be, and the same are hereby pledged and appropriated for the payment of the payment of the annuity stipulated in the said Treaty to be paid to the sais Dey and Regency of Algiers; and to continue so pledged and appropriated, so long as the said treaty shall be in force.

Approved May 6, 1796

THE HUMILIATION OF COMMODORE BAINBRIDGE BY BOBBA MUSTAPHA

Be it further Enacted by the authority aforesaid, that no person being an African or Negroe, other than a subject of the Emperor of *Morocco*, or a citizen of some one of the United States; to be evidenced by a certificate from the Secretary of the State of which he shall be a citizen, shall tarry within this Commonwealth, for a longer time than two months, & upon complaint made to any Justice of the Peace within this Commonwealth, that any such person has been within the same more than two months, the said Justice shall order the said person to depart out of this Commonwealth, & in case that the said African or Negroe shall not depart as aforesaid, any Justice of the Peace within this Commonwealth, upon complaint & proof made that such person has continued within this Commonwealth ten days after notice given him or her to depart as aforesaid, shall commit the said person to any house of correction within the County, there to be kept to hard labour agreeably to the rules & orders of the said house, until the sessions of the peace, next to be holden within & for the said County; and the master of the said house of correction is hereby required & directed to transmit an attested copy of the warrant of commitment to the said Court, on the first day of their said Session, & if upon trial at the said Court, it shall be made to appear that the said person has thus continued within the Commonwealth contrary to the tenor of this Act, he or she shall be whipped not exceeding ten stripes, and ordered to depart out of this Commonwealth within ten days; and if he or she shall not so depart, the same process shall be had and punishment inflicted, and so *toties quoties.*

March 26, 1788.

Mr. and Mrs. John Jones, two prominent free-born "Negros" of Chicago. Although they were free, they complied with Illinois law that required free blacks and mulattos to obtain a certificate of freedom and to post a $1,000 bond for the privilege of traveling and living in the state (below). When blacks became eligible to hold office in 1869, Governor John M. Palmer appointed Mr. Jones a notary public for the state, making him the first black in that post. Later, in 1871, he was elected a Cook County commissioner, becoming the first black elected to public office in Chicago. After his one year term was over, he was reelected for a three-year term.

The Barbary Treaties 1786-1816
Treaty with Morocco June 28 and July 15, 1786

Treaty of Peace and Friendship, with additional article; also Ship-Signals Agreement. The treaty was sealed at Morocco with the seal of the Emperor of Morocco June 23, 1786 (25 Shaban, A. H. 1200), and delivered to Thomas Barclay, American Agent, June 28, 1786 (1 Ramadan, A. H. 1200). Original in Arabic. The additional article was signed and sealed at Morocco on behalf of Morocco July 15, 1786 (18 Ramadan, A. H. 1200). Original in Arabic. The Ship-Signals Agreement was signed at Morocco July 6, 1786 (9 Ramadan, A. H. 1200). Original in English.

Certified English translations of the treaty and of the additional article were incorporated in a document signed and sealed by the Ministers Plenipotentiary of the United States, Thomas Jefferson at Paris January 1, 1787, and John Adams at London January 25, 1787.

Treaty and additional article ratified by the United States July 18, 1787. As to the ratification generally, see the notes. Treaty and additional article proclaimed July 18, 1787.

Ship-Signals Agreement not specifically included in the ratification and not proclaimed; but copies ordered by Congress July 23, 1787, to be sent to the Executives of the States (Secret Journals of Congress, IV, 869; but see the notes as to this reference).

[Certified Translation of the Treaty and of the Additional Article, with Approval by Jefferson and Adams]

To all Persons to whom these Presents shall come or be made known- Whereas the United States of America in Congress assembled by their Commission bearing date the twelvth day of May One thousand Seven hundred and Eighty four thought proper to constitute John Adams, Benjamin Franklin and Thomas Jefferson their Ministers Plenipotentiary, giving to them or a Majority of them full Powers to confer, treat & negotiate with the Ambassador, Minister or Commissioner of His Majesty the Emperor of Morocco concerning a Treaty of Amity and Commerce, to make & receive propositions for such Treaty and to conclude and sign the same, transmitting it to the United States in Congress assembled for their final Ratification, And by one other commission bearing date the Eleventh day of March One thousand Seven hundred & Eighty five did further empower the said Ministers Plenipotentiary or a majority of them, by writing under the hands and Seals to appoint such Agent in the said Business as they might think proper with Authority under the directions and instructions of the said Ministers to commence & prosecute the said Negotiations & Conferences for the said Treaty provided that the said Treaty should be signed by the said Ministers: And Whereas, We the said John Adams & Thomas Jefferson two of the said Ministers Plenipotentiary (the said Benjamin Franklin being absent) by writing under the Hand and Seal of the said John Adams at London October the fifth, One thousand Seven hundred and Eighty five, & of the said Thomas Jefferson at Paris October the Eleventh of the same Year, did appoint Thomas Barclay, Agent in the Business aforesaid, giving him the Powers therein, which by the said second Commission we were authorized to give, and the said Thomas Barclay in pursuance thereof, hath arranged Articles for a Treaty of Amity and Commerce between the United States of America and His Majesty the Emperor of Morocco, which Articles written in the Arabic Language, confirmed by His said Majesty the Emperor of Morocco & seal'd with His Royal Seal, being translated into the Language of the said United States of America, together with the Attestations thereto annexed are in the following Words, To Wit.

In the name of Almighty God,

This is a Treaty of Peace and Friendship established between us and the United States of America, which is confirmed, and which we have ordered to be written in this Book and sealed with our Royal Seal at our Court of Morocco on the twenty fifth day of the blessed Month of Shaban, in the Year One thousand two hundred, trusting in God it will remain permanent.

.1.

We declare that both Parties have agreed that this Treaty consisting of twenty five Articles shall be inserted in this Book and delivered to the Honorable Thomas Barclay, the Agent of the United States now at our Court, with whose Approbation it has been made and who is duly authorized on their Part, to treat with us concerning all the Matters contained therein.

.2.

If either of the Parties shall be at War with any Nation whatever, the other Party shall not take a Commission from the Enemy nor fight under their Colors.

.3.

If either of the Parties shall be at War with any Nation whatever and take a Prize belonging to that Nation, and there shall be found on board Subjects or Effects belonging to either of the Parties, the Subjects shall be set at Liberty and the Effects returned to the Owners. And if any Goods belonging to any Nation, with whom either of the Parties shall be at War, shall be loaded on Vessels belonging to the other Party, they shall pass free and unmolested without any attempt being made to take or detain them.

.4.

A Signal or Pass shall be given to all Vessels belonging to both Parties, by which they are to be known when they meet at Sea, and if the Commander of a Ship of War of either Party shall have other Ships under his Convoy, the Declaration of the Commander shall alone be sufficient to exempt any of them from examination.

.5.

If either of the Parties shall be at War, and shall meet a Vessel at Sea, belonging to the other, it is agreed that if an examination is to be made, it shall be done by sending a Boat with two or three Men only, and if any Gun shall be fired and injury done without Reason, the offending Party shall make good all damages.

.6.

If any Moor shall bring Citizens of the United States or their Effects to His Majesty, the Citizens shall immediately be set at Liberty and the Effects restored, and in like Manner, if any Moor not a Subject of these Dominions shall make Prize of any of the Citizens of America or their Effects and bring them into any of the Ports of His Majesty, they shall be immediately released, as they will then be considered as under His Majesty's Protection.

.7.

If any Vessel of either Party shall put into a Port of the other and have occasion for Provisions or other Supplies, they shall be furnished without any interruption or molestation.

If any Vessel of the United States shall meet with a Disaster at Sea and put into one of our Ports to repair, she shall be at Liberty to land and reload her cargo, without paying any Duty whatever.

.9.

If any Vessel of the United States shall be cast on Shore on any Part of our Coasts, she shall remain at the disposition of the Owners and no one shall attempt going near her without their Approbation, as she is then considered particularly under our Protection; and if any Vessel of the United States shall be forced to put into our Ports, by Stress of weather or otherwise, she shall not be compelled to land her Cargo, but shall remain in tranquility until the Commander shall think proper to proceed on his Voyage.

.10.

If any Vessel of either of the Parties shall have an engagement with a Vessel belonging to any of the Christian Powers within gunshot of the Forts of the other, the Vessel so engaged shall be defended and protected as much as possible until she is in safety; And if any American Vessel shall be cast on shore on the Coast of Wadnoon [1] or any coast thereabout, the People belonging to her shall be protected, and assisted until by the help of God, they shall be sent to their Country.

.11.

If we shall be at War with any Christian Power and any of our Vessels sail from the Ports of the United States, no Vessel belonging to the enemy shall follow until twenty four hours after the Departure of our Vessels; and the same Regulation shall be observed towards the American Vessels sailing from our Ports.-be their enemies Moors or Christians.

.12.

If any Ship of War belonging to the United States shall put into any of our Ports, she shall not be examined on any Pretence whatever, even though she should have fugitive Slaves on Board, nor shall the Governor or Commander of the Place compel them to be brought on Shore on any pretext, nor require any payment for them.

.13.

If a Ship of War of either Party shall put into a Port of the other and salute, it shall be returned from the Fort, with an equal Number of Guns, not with more or less.

.14.

The Commerce with the United States shall be on the same footing as is the Commerce with Spain or as that with the most favored Nation for the time being and their Citizens shall be respected and esteemed and have full Liberty to pass and repass our Country and Sea Ports whenever they please without interruption.

.15.

Merchants of both Countries shall employ only such Interpreters, & such other Persons to assist them in their Business, as they shall think proper. No Commander of a Vessel shall transport his Cargo on board another Vessel, he shall not be detained in Port, longer than he may think proper, and all persons employed in loading or unloading Goods or in any other Labor whatever, shall be paid at the Customary rates, not more and not less.

.16.

In case of a War between the Parties, the Prisoners are not to be made Slaves, but to be exchanged one for another, Captain for Captain, Officer for Officer and one private Man for another; and if there shall prove a deficiency on either side, it shall be made up by the payment of one hundred

Mexican Dollars for each Person wanting; And it is agreed that all Prisoners shall be exchanged in twelve Months from the Time of their being taken, and that this exchange may be effected by a Merchant or any other Person authorized by either of the Parties.

.17.

Merchants shall not be compelled to buy or Sell any kind of Goods but such as they shall think proper; and may buy and sell all sorts of Merchandise but such as are prohibited to the other Christian Nations.

.18.

All goods shall be weighed and examined before they are sent on board, and to avoid all detention of Vessels, no examination shall afterwards be made, unless it shall first be proved, that contraband Goods have been sent on board, in which Case the Persons who took the contraband Goods on board shall be punished according to the Usage and Custom of the Country and no other Person whatever shall be injured, nor shall the Ship or Cargo incur any Penalty or damage whatever.

.19.

No vessel shall be detained in Port on any presence whatever, nor be obliged to take on board any Article without the consent of the Commander, who shall be at full Liberty to agree for the Freight of any Goods he takes on board.

.20.

If any of the Citizens of the United States, or any Persons under their Protection, shall have any disputes with each other, the Consul shall decide between the Parties and whenever the Consul shall require any Aid or Assistance from our Government to enforce his decisions it shall be immediately granted to him.

.21.

If a Citizen of the United States should kill or wound a Moor, or on the contrary if a Moor shall kill or wound a Citizen of the United States, the Law of the Country shall take place and equal Justice shall be rendered, the Consul assisting at the Tryal, and if any Delinquent shall make his escape, the Consul shall not be answerable for him in any manner whatever.

.22.

If an American Citizen shall die in our Country and no Will shall appear, the Consul shall take possession of his Effects, and if there shall be no Consul, the Effects shall be deposited in the hands of some Person worthy of Trust, untill the Party shall appear who has a Right to demand them, but if the Heir to the Person deceased be present, the Property shall be delivered to him without interruption; and if a Will shall appear, the Property shall descend agreeable to that Will, as soon as the Consul shall declare the Validity thereof.

.23.

The Consuls of the United States of America shall reside in any Sea Port of our Dominions that they shall think proper; And they shall be respected and enjoy all the Privileges which the Consuls of any other Nation enjoy, and if any of the Citizens of the United States shall contract any Debts or engagements, the Consul shall not be in any Manner accountable for them, unless he shall have given a Promise in writing for the payment or fulfilling thereof, without which promise in Writing no Application to him for any redress shall be made.

.24.

If any differences shall arise by either Party infringing on any of the Articles of this Treaty, Peace and Harmony shall remain notwithstanding in the fullest force, untill a friendly Application shall be made for an Arrangement, and untill that Application shall be rejected, no appeal shall be made to Arms. And if a War shall break out between the Parties, Nine Months shall be granted to all the Subjects of both Parties, to dispose of their Effects and retire with their Property. And it is further declared that whatever Indulgences in Trade or otherwise shall be granted to any of the Christian Powers, the Citizens of the United States shall be equally entitled to them.

.25.

This Treaty shall continue in full Force, with the help of God for Fifty Years.

We have delivered this Book into the Hands of the before-mentioned Thomas Barclay on the first day of the blessed Month of Ramadan, in the Year One thousand two hundred.

I certify that the annex'd is a true Copy of the Translation made by Issac Cardoza Nunez, Interpreter at Morocco, of the treaty between the Emperor of Morocco and the United States of America.

THOS BARCLAY

(1) Or Ouadnoun, on the Atlantic coast, about latitude 29° N. Back

Source:
Treaties and Other International Acts of the United States of America.
Edited by Hunter Miller
Volume 2
Documents 1-40 : 1776-1818
Washington : Government Printing Office, 1931.

The Barbary Treaties 1786-1816
Treaty with Morocco June 28 and July 15, 1786 - Translation of the Additional Article

Grace to the only God

I the underwritten the Servant of God, Taher Ben Abdelhack Fennish do certify that His Imperial Majesty my Master /whom God preserve/ having concluded a Treaty of Peace and Commerce with the United States of America has ordered me the better to compleat it and in addition of the tenth Article of the Treaty to declare " That,

"if any Vessel belonging to the United States shall be in any of the
"Ports of His Majesty's Dominions, or within Gunshot of his Forts,
"she shall be protected as much as possible and no Vessel whatever
"belonging either to Moorish or Christian Powers with whom the
"United States may be at War, shall be permitted to follow or engage
"her, as we now deem the Citizens of America our good Friends.

And in obedience to His Majesty's Commands I certify this Declaration by putting my hand and Seal to it, on the Eighteenth day of Ramadan in the Year One thousand two hundred.

(Signed)

The Servant of the fling my Master whom God preserve
TAMER BEN ABDELHACK(1) FENNISH

I Do Certify that the above is a True Copy of the Translation Made at Morocco by Isaac Cardoza Nunes, Interpreter, of a Declaration Made and Signed by Sidi Hage Tahar Fennish in addition to the Treaty between the Emperor of Morocco and the United States of America which Declaration the said Tahar Fennish Made by the Express Directions of His Majesty.

THos BARCLAY

Note, The Ramadan of the Year of the Hegira 1200 Commenced on the 28th June in the Year of our Lord 1786.

Now know Ye that We the said John Adams & Thomas Jefferson Ministers Plenipotentiary aforesaid do approve & conclude the said Treaty and every Article and Clause therein contained, reserving the same nevertheless to the United States in Congress assembled for their final Ratification.

In testimony whereof we have signed the same with our Names and Seals, at the places of our respective residence and at the dates expressed under our signatures respectively.

John ADAMS. [Seal]

LONDON January 25, 1787.

TH: JEFFERSON [Seal]

PARIS January 1, 1787.

(1) The spelling in the original document is uncertain, but Abdelhack is correct, el-Hack or el-Haqq being one of the names of God. Back

Source:
Treaties and Other International Acts of the United States of America.
Edited by Hunter Miller
Volume 2
Documents 1-40 : 1776-1818
Washington : Government Printing Office, 1931.

on their late visit to the seat of Congress and that the expences attending the same be allowed.

d° *Resolved* That all communications to the United States in Congress from the Indian tribes ought to be made through the Superintendants of Indian Affairs.

d° *Resolved* That if any trader or other person shall without the Authority of the said Superintendants undertake to conduct any Indian or Indians to the seat of Congress, he shall be responsible for all expences which may attend the same; and further that where the person so acting as a conductor shall be a trader, his license to trade with the said Indians shall become forfeited and the same shall at no time thereafter be renewed.

d° *Resolved* That the superintendants of Indian Affairs be instructed to make public the foregoing resolutions and to govern themselves accordingly.

[1] On a report [2] from the Secretary for foreign Affairs to whom was referred a treaty [3] lately concluded with the Emperor of Morocco, Congress ratified the said treaty in the manner and form following.

The United States of America in Congress assembled to all who shall see these presents, Greeting

Whereas the United States of America in Congress assembled by their commission bearing date the twelfth day of

---

[1] From this point to the end of the treaty, the proceedings, excepting the text of the treaty, are also entered by John Fisher and attested by Charles Thomson, in the *Secret Journal Foreign, Papers of the Continental Congress*, No. 6, III, pp. 377–380. They are also entered by Thomson in *Secret Journal, Foreign Affairs, Papers of the Continental Congress*, No. 5, III, pp. 1616–1619.

[2] Read May 8, 1787. See April 12, 1787.

[3] The original translation, certified by Thomas Barclay and ratified by John Adams and Thomas Jefferson, is in *Papers of the Continental Congress*, No. 91, pp. 215–229. A printed copy of the treaty, signed by Charles Thomson, is in *Papers of the Continental Congress*, Broadsides. See Hunter Miller, *Treaties and other International Acts of the United States of America*, vol. II, pp. 186–218.

United States of America together with the attestations thereto annexed are in the following words, to wit,

"In the name of Almighty God

This is a treaty of peace and friendship established between Us and the United States of America which is confirmed and which we have ordered to be written in this book and sealed with our royal seal at our court of Morocco on the twenty fifth day of the blessed Month of Shaban, in the year one thousand two hundred trusting in God it will remain permanent.

1. We declare that both parties have agreed that this treaty consisting of twenty five Articles shall be inserted in this book and delivered to the honorable Thomas Barclay the agent of the United States now at our court, with whose approbation it has been made and who is duly authorised on their part to treat with us concerning all the matters contained therein.

2. If either of the parties shall be at war with any nation whatever, the other party shall not take a commission from the enemy nor fight under their colours.

3. If either of the parties shall be at war with any nation whatever and take a prize belonging to that nation and there shall be found on board subjects or effects belonging to either of the parties, the subjects shall be set at liberty and the effects returned to the Owners. And if any goods belonging to any nation with whom either of the parties shall be at war shall be loaded on vessels belonging to the other party, they shall pass free and unmolested without any attempt being made to take or detain them.

4. A signal or pass shall be given to all vessels belonging to both parties by which they are to be known when they meet at sea, and if the Commander of a ship of war of either party shall have other ships under his convoy the declaration of

the Commander shall alone be sufficient to exempt any of them from examination.

5. If either of the parties shall be at war and shall meet a vessel at sea belonging to the other it is agreed that if an examination is to be made, it shall be done by sending a boat with two or three men only and if any gun shall be fired and injury done without reason the offending party shall make good all damages.

6. If any Moor shall bring citizens of the United States or their effects to his Majesty, the citizens shall immediately be set at liberty and the effects restored and in like manner, if any Moor not a subject of these dominions shall make prize of any of the citizens of America or their effects and bring them into any of the ports of his Majesty they shall be immediately released as they will then be considered as under his Majesty's protection.

7. If any vessel of either party shall put into a port of the other and have occasion for provisions or other supplies they shall be furnished without any interruption or molestation.

8. If any vessel of the United States shall meet with a disaster at sea and put into one of our ports to repair she shall be at liberty to land and reload her cargo without paying any duty whatever.

9. If any vessel of the United States shall be cast[1] on shore on any part of our Coasts, she shall remain at the disposition of the owners, and no one shall attempt going near her without their approbation as she is then considered particularly under our protection; and if any Vessel of the United States shall be forced to put into our ports by stress of weather or otherwise, she shall not be compelled to land her Cargo, but shall remain in tranquility until the commander shall think proper to proceed on his Voyage.

[1] At this point John Fisher takes up the entry.

10. If any Vessel of either of the parties shall have an engagement with a Vessel belonging to any of the Christian powers within gun shot of the forts of the other, the Vessel so engaged shall be defended and protected as much as possible until she is in safety; and if any American Vessel shall be cast on shore on the coast of Wadnoon or any Coast thereabout, the people belonging to her shall be protected and assisted until by the help of God they shall be sent to their Country.

11. If we shall be at war with any christian power, and any of our Vessels sail from the ports of the United States, no Vessel belonging to the enemy shall follow, until twenty four hours after the departure of our Vessels, and the same regulation shall be observed towards the American Vessels sailing from our ports;—be their enemies Moors or Christians.

12. If any Ship of war belonging to the United States shall put into any of our ports, she shall not be examined on any pretence whatever, even though she should have fugitive slaves on board, nor shall the Governor or Commander of the place compel them to be brought on shore on any pretext, nor require any payment for them.

13. If a Ship of war of either party shall put into a port of the other, and Salute, it shall be returned from the Fort with an equal number of guns, not with more or less.

14. The Commerce with the United States shall be on the same footing as is the Commerce with Spain, or as that with the most favored Nation for the time being, and their Citizens shall be respected and esteemed, and have full liberty to pass and repass our Country and Sea ports whenever they please without interruption.

15. Merchants of both Countries shall employ only such interpreters, and such other persons to assist them in their business as they shall think proper. No commander of a

Vessel shall transport his Cargo on board another Vessel, he shall not be detained in port longer than he may think proper, and all persons employed in loading and unloading goods or in any other labor whatever shall be paid at the customary rates, not more and not less.

16. In case of a war between the parties, the prisoners are not to be made slaves, but to be exchanged one for another, Captain for Captain, Officer for Officer and one private man for another; and if there shall prove a deficiency on either side it shall be made up by the payment of one hundred Mexican dollars for each person wanting; And it is agreed that all prisoners shall be exchanged in twelve months from the time of their being taken, and that this exchange may be effected by a merchant, or any other person authorized by either of the parties.

17. Merchants shall not be compelled to buy or sell any kind of goods, but such as they shall think proper, and may buy and sell all sorts of merchandize but such as are prohibited to the other Christian Nations.

18. All goods shall be weighed and examined before they are sent on board, and to avoid all detention of Vessels no examination shall afterwards be made, unless it shall first be proved, that contraband goods have been sent on board, in which case the persons who took the contraband goods on board shall be punished according to the usage and custom of the Country, and no other person whatever shall be injured, nor shall the ship or cargo incur any penalty or damage whatever.

19. No Vessel shall be detained in port on any pretence whatever, nor be obliged to take on board any Article without the consent of the commander who shall be at full liberty to agree for the freight of any goods he takes on board.

20. If any of the Citizens of the United States or any persons under their protection shall have any disputes with

each other, the Consul shall decide between the parties and whenever the consul shall require any aid or assistance from our government to enforce his decisions it shall be immediately granted to him.

21. If a Citizen of the United States should kill or wound a Moor or on the contrary if a Moor shall kill or wound a Citizen of the United States, the law of the Country shall take place, and equal justice shall be rendered, the Consul assisting at the trial, and if any delinquent shall make his escape, the consul shall not be answerable for him in any manner whatever.

22. If an American Citizen shall die in our Country and no Will shall appear, the Consul shall take possession of his Effects, and if there shall be no consul, the Effects shall be deposited in the hands of some person worthy of trust, until the party shall appear who has a right to demand them, but if the Heir to the person deceased be present, the property shall be delivered to him without interruption; and if a will shall appear, the property shall descend agreeable to that will as soon as the Consul shall declare the Validity thereof.

23. The Consuls of the United States of America shall reside in any sea port of our Dominions that they shall think proper; and they shall be respected and enjoy all the privileges which the Consuls of any other Nation enjoy, and if any of the Citizens of the United States shall contract any Debts or engagements, the Consul shall not be in any manner accountable for them, unless he shall have given a promise in writing, for the payment or fulfilling thereof, without which promise in writing no application to him for any redress shall be made.

24. If any differences shall arise by either party infringing on any of the Articles of this treaty, peace and harmony shall remain notwithstanding in the fullest force, until a friendly

application shall be made for an arrangement, and until that application shall be rejected, no appeal shall be made to arms. And if a war shall break out between the parties, nine months shall be granted to all the Subjects of both parties to dispose of their effects and retire with their property. And it is further declared that whatever indulgences in trade or otherwise shall be granted to any of the Christian powers, the Citizens of the United States shall be equally entitled to them.

25. This Treaty shall continue in full force with the help of God for fifty years.

We have delivered this Book into the hands of the beforementioned Thomas Barclay on the first day of the blessed month of Ramadan in the year one thousand two hundred.

I certify that the annexed is a true copy of the translation made by Isaac Cardoza Nunez, Interpreter at Morocco, of the Treaty between the Emperor of Morocco and the United States of America.

(Signed) THOˢ BARCLAY

Additional Article

Grace to the only God.

I the under written, the servant of God, Taher Ben Abdelkack Tennish, do certify that his Imperial Majesty my master (whom God preserve) having concluded a treaty of peace and Commerce with the United States of America, has ordered me the better to compleat it, and in addition to the tenth Article of the treaty to declare "That if any vessel belonging to the United States shall be in any of the ports of His Majesty's dominions, or within gun shot of his forts, she shall be protected as much as possible and no Vessel whatever belonging either to Moorish or Christian powers with whom the United States may be at war shall be permitted to follow or engage her as we now deem the Citizens of America our good friends."

July, 1787

And in obedience to his Majesty's Command, I certify this declaration by putting my hand and seal to it, on the eighteenth day of Ramadan in the year one thousand two hundred.
(Signed)
The Servant of the King my master whom God preserve
TAHER BEN ABDELKACK TENNISH

[1] I do certify that the above is a true copy of the translation made at Morocco by Isaac Cordoza Nunez, interpreter of a declaration made and signed by Sidi Hage Taher Fennish in addition to the treaty between the Emperor of Morocco and the United States of America which declaration the said Taher Fennish made by the Express directions of his Majesty
(signed) THOMAS BARCLAY." [2]

And Whereas the said John Adams and Thomas Jefferson Ministers plenipotentiary aforesaid by writing under their respective hands and seals duly made and executed by the said John Adams on the 25th January 1787, and by the said Thomas Jefferson on the 1st day of January 1787, did approve and conclude the said Treaty and every Article and clause therein contained, reserving the same nevertheless to the United States in Congress Assembled for their final ratification. Now be it Known that we the said United States of America in Congress Assembled, have accepted, approved, ratified and confirmed, and by these presents do accept, approve, ratify, and confirm the said Treaty and every Article and clause thereof.

In testimony whereof we have caused our Seal to be hereunto affixed. Witness his Excellency Arthur St Clair our President, at the City of New-York, this 18th day of July in

---

[1] This paragraph is in the writing of Charles Thomson.
[2] The original ratification of Adams and Jefferson, which follows at this point, was not incorporated in the ratification by Congress.

the year of our Lord 1787, and in the twelfth year of our Sovereignty and Independence.

[1] *Ordered* That the Secretary for foreign Affairs prepare the draught of a letter to the Emperor of Morocco to accompany the ratification of the treaty with his Majesty.[2]

CHA^s THOMSON *Sec^y*

Ordered That the Secretary for foreign Affairs prepare the draught of a letter of thanks to his Catholic Majesty for his good Offices in promoting a treaty between the United States of America and the Emperor of Morocco.[2]

CHA^s THOMSON *Sec^y*

On a report [3] of the Secretary of the United States for the department of foreign Affairs to whom was referred a petition [4] from Hannah Stephens praying that her Husband be redeemed from Captivity at Algiers, and also a letter [5] from the Honorable T. Jefferson proposing that a certain order of priests be employed for such purposes.

Resolved That the Honorable T. Jefferson Esquire the minister of the United States at the Court of Versailles be, and he hereby is authorised to take such measures

---

[1] From this point to the end of the day the proceedings are entered by John Fisher and attested by Charles Thomson in *Secret Journal Foreign, Papers of the Continental Congress,* No. 6, pp. 380 and 376–377. The orders referring to the Moroccan treaty are also entered by Thomson in *Secret Journal, Foreign Affairs, Papers of the Continental Congress,* No. 5, p. 1619 and the proceedings regarding Hannah Stephens, by Benjamin Bankson, *ibid,* pp. 1612–1613 and on margin of p. 1618.

[2] These two orders are noted as referred to the Secretary for Foreign Affairs in the *Committee Book, Papers of the Continental Congress,* No. 190, p. 153. Report was rendered July 23, 1787.

[3] See May 2, 1787.

[4] See April 23, 1787.

[5] Dated February 1, 1787. See April 18, 1787.

Cadran the transmission of the Marqs. de la Fayette's letters for Mr. Crevecœur through my hands, was very acceptable to me and did not stand in need of an apology.

About the time I was occupied in forwarding the Packet to New York, I had the satisfaction to hear of Mr. Warville's[54] safe arrival in Boston. From the favorable character given of that Gentleman, and the important object which has occasioned his advent, I hope his visit to America may become equally interesting and satisfactory in a personal and national point of view.[55] With sentiments of esteem etc.[56]

To DOCTOR THOMAS THOMSON[57]

Mount Vernon, August 21, 1788.

Sir: In answer to your favor of the 12th. instant, I can assure you, if it shall be found that Doctr. Spence[58] and family are in the unhappy situation you suppose, and I can be instrumental by writing to Mr. Jefferson or to any of my friends in France in obtaining their release, I should do it with cheerfulness and pleasure. An application to the Court of that Nation from a private character would be improper, such, if made, ought to go from the Sovereignty of these States.

But, Sir, let not Mr. Thomson's hopes on this occasion be too sanguine. There are reasons to distrust the narrative of James Joshua Reynolds; to denominate him an Imposter (as you will

---

[54] J. P. Brissot de Warville.
[55] Warville visited Mount Vernon, Nov. 15–17, 1788, and described his visit in his *Nouveau Voyage dans les État Unis de l'Amérique Septentrionale, fait en 1788*, which was published in Paris in 1791.
[56] From the "Letter Book" copy in the *Washington Papers*.
On August 18 Washington wrote briefly to Marquis de Lotbiniere, acknowledging his congratulations on the ratification of the Constitution by New York; and to a Monsieur Cadran, thanking him for forwarding letters. Copies of both these letters are in the "Letter Book" in the *Washington Papers*.
[57] Of Nomini, Westmoreland County, Va.
[58] Dr. William Spence.

perceive by the enclosed transcript from the Pensyla. Packet and Daily Advertiser) and other informations which your Son will probably communicate to you; and that the accounts given by this Reynolds are for time Serving purposes. To these in my opinion, may be added, as strengthing the evidence, of Doctor Spences own letter dated within a few days Sail off Sandy hook where it is believed no Cruiser from the Piratical State ever yet appeared none having ever yet been seen, or heard to be, in these Seas. If therefore it was his fate to fall into the hands of these pests to mankind it must have been by Re-capture which is not very probable from the accts. that are delivered.

The most eligable previous steps in this business, in my judgment, will be, to write first to Mr. Barclay,[59] who has not been long returned from the court of Morocco in a public character and particularly from Algiers, and who must have obtained the *best* information of all American Prisoners, at least of the capture of the Vessels in which they were; to know if any such information ever came before him, and at the same time to enquire more particular of some Gentlemen in Philadelphia with respect to this Reynolds, the circumstances related by him of the Vessel called the Rising Sun of Israel Jacobs &c. These I will do, the answers may throw light upon the subject and direct what further Measures may be necessary to pursue when I receive them, the Result shall be communicated to you, by Sir Yr. etc.[60]

To JOHN FITZGERALD AND GEORGE GILPIN

Mount Vernon, August 22, 1788.

Gentlemen: It is of so much consequence to the Company, that *necessary* and *legal* measures should be pursued to obtain

---
[59] Thomas Barclay.
[60] From the "Letter Book" copy in the *Washington Papers*.

Your observations upon the necessity there is for good dispositions to prevail among the Gentlemen of Congress, are extremely just; and hitherto, everything seems to promise that the good effects which are expected from an accommodating and conciliating spirit in that body, will not be frustrated.

That part of the President's duty which obliges him to nominate persons for offices is the most delicate, and in many instances will be, to me, the most unpleasing; for it may frequently happen that there will be several applicants for the same office, whose merits and pretensions are so nearly equal that it will almost require the aid of supernatural intuition to fix upon the right. I shall, however, in all events, have the consolation of knowing that I entered upon my office unconfined by engagements, and uninfluenced by any ties; and that no means in my power will be left untried to find out, and nominate those characters who will discharge the duties of their respective offices to the best interest and highest credit of the American Union.

I cannot close this letter, my dear Sir, without thanking you very sincerely for your friendly sentiments and good wishes; and beg you will be assured that I am etc.[93] [N.Y.P.L.]

To GOVERNOR BEVERLEY RANDOLPH

New York, May 16, 1789.

Sir: A letter of the 4th instant from Lt: Governor Wood[94] has been received with its inclosures, containing the information of some murders committed by the Indians on the 23d of last month at Dunkard Creek which runs into the Monongahala River.

It is with great concern that I learn this circumstance, as a treaty has been lately concluded by the Governor of the western

---
[93] In the writing of Tobias Lear.
[94] James Wood, Lieutenant Governor of Virginia.

territory with the Wiandot, Delawar, Ottawa, Chippawa, Pattawatima, and Sac nations of Indians, North West of the Ohio.

It is most probable that the recent murders have been committed by a party from the remnants of the Shawanese tribe, who are joined by a few renegado Cherokees.

The Governor of the western territory,[95] who is here, will soon return to the frontiers, and he will, in conjunction with the commanding officer of the troops, take such measures, with the said Shawanese and other refractory tribes, as the occasion may require, and the public situation admit.

It would be highly proper, in future, in case of depredations south of the Ohio, that information be communicated as early as possible to the nearest post of the troops stationed on the Ohio, in order if possible that the banditii be intercepted. I have the honor etc.[96] [H.S.P.]

To MARY WOOSTER [97]

New York, May 21, 1789.

Madam: I have duly received your affecting letter, dated the 8th day of this Month.[98] Sympathizing with you, as I do, in the great misfortunes, which have befallen your family in consequence of the War; my feelings as an individual would forcibly prompt me to do every thing in my power to repair those misfortunes. But as a public man, acting only with a reference to the public good, I must be allowed to decide upon all points of my duty without consulting my private inclinations and wishes. I must be permitted, with the best lights I can obtain, and upon a general view of characters and circumstances,

---

[95] Arthur St. Clair.
[96] In the writing of Tobias Lear.
[97] Widow of Brig. Gen. David Wooster.
[98] Mrs. Wooster's letter, requesting for the appointment of her son Thomas, is in the *Applications for Office under Washington* in the Library of Congress.

acceptable Persons; and having reason to believe that the appointments which have been made heretofore have given very general satisfaction it would give me pain if Mr. Wythe or any of his friends should conceive that he has been passed by from improper motives. I have prejudices against none, nor partialities which shall bias me in favor of any one. If I err then, my errors will be of the head and not of the heart of my dear Sir, your most obedient &c.[81]

To THE EMPEROR OF MOROCCO

City of New York, December 1, 1789.

Great and Magnanimous Friend: Since the Date of the Letter which the late Congress, by their President, addressed to your Imperial Majesty, the United States of America have thought proper to change their Government, and to institute a new one, agreeable to the Constitution, of which I have the Honor of, herewith, enclosing a Copy. The Time necessarily employed in the arduous Task, and the Derangements occasioned by so great, though peaceable a Revolution, will apologize, and account for your Majesty's not having received those regular Advices, and Marks of Attention, from the United States, which the Friendship and Magnanimity of your Conduct, towards them, afforded Reason to expect.

The United States, having unanimously appointed me to the supreme executive Authority, in this Nation, your Majesty's Letter of the 17th: August 1788, which by Reason of the Disso-

---

[81] From the "Letter Book" copy in the *Washington Papers*.
On December 23 Randolph wrote to Washington: "I found a fortunate moment for a conversation with Mr. Wythe. He repeated what I wrote to you in answer to your favor of the 30th. Ulto. Indeed he declared himself happy in believing, that he held a place in your esteem; and that he was confident, you had looked towards him with every partiality, which he could wish. Nay without going into the detail of our discourse, I am convinced from his own mouth, that the knowledge of his present situation is considered by him, as the only reason of a seat on the bench, not being tendered to him." Randolph's letter is in the *Washington Papers*.

lution of the late Government, remained unanswered, has been delivered to me. I have also received the Letters which your Imperial Majesty has been so kind as to write, in favor of the United States, to the Bashaws of Tunis and Tripoli, and I present to you the sincere Acknowledgments and Thanks of the United States, for this important Mark of your Friendship for them.

We greatly regret that the hostile Disposition of those Regencies, towards this Nation, who have never injured them, is not to be removed, on Terms in our Power to comply with. Within our Territories there are no Mines, either of Gold, or Silver, and this young Nation, just recovering from the Waste and Desolation of a long War, have not, as yet, had Time to acquire Riches by Agriculture and Commerce. But our Soil is boundtiful, and our People industrious; and we have Reason to flatter ourselves, that we shall gradually become useful to our Friends.

The Encouragement which your Majesty has been pleased, generously, to give to our Commerce with your Dominions; the Punctuality with which you have caused the Treaty with us to be observed; and the just and generous Measures taken in the Case of Captain Proctor,[52] make a deep Impression on the United States, and confirm their Respect for, and Attachment to your Imperial Majesty.

It gives me Pleasure to have this Opportunity of assuring your Majesty that, while I remain at the Head of this Nation, I shall not cease to promote every Measure that may conduce to the Friendship and Harmony, which so happily subsist between your Empire and them, and shall esteem myself happy in every

---

[52] Apparently some inadvertence, as Thomas Jefferson, writing from Paris (Sept. 9, 1789) to Giuseppe Chiappe, speaks of the release of the schooner *Proctor* by the Emperor. A press copy of this letter is in the *Jefferson Papers* in the Library of Congress.

Occasion of convincing your Majesty of the high Sense (which in common with the whole Nation) I entertain of the Magnanimity, Wisdom, and Benevolence of your Majesty. In the Course of the approaching Winter, the national Legislature (which is called by the former Name of Congress) will assemble, and I shall take Care that Nothing be omitted that may be necessary to cause the Correspondence, between our Countries, to be maintained and conducted in a Manner agreeable to your Majesty, and satisfactory to all the Parties concerned in it.

May the Almighty bless your Imperial Majesty, our great and magnanimous Friend, with his constant Guidance and Protection.[53]

To ROBERT MORRIS

New York, December 14, 1789.

Dear Sir: I have been favored with the receipt of your letter of the 9th instant.[54] In reply to the object of its enclosure, I can

---

[53] From a photostat of the original kindly furnished by George A. Ball, of Muncie, Ind.

On December 1 the New Jersey Legislature sent an address to Washington, whose reply, undated, is recorded in the "Letter Book" immediately following the copy of the address. In the reply Washington wrote: "The opportunities, which were afforded me in the trying vicissitudes of our arduous struggle, to remark the generous spirit, which animated the exertions of your citizens, have impressed a remembrance of their worth, which no length of time or change of circumstances can efface. . . . In making my acknowledgments for the favorable opinions you express of my military conduct, as it respected the observance of civil rights, it is but justice to assign great merit to the temper of those citizens, whose estates were more immediately the scene of warfare. Their personal services were rendered without constraint, and the derangement of their affairs submitted to without dissatisfaction. It was the triumph of patriotism over personal considerations. And our present enjoyments of peace and freedom reward the sacrifice."

On December 4 Lear wrote to William Duer, that Washington would "keep the Carriage provided for his use previous to his arrival in New York . . . as it will be considered upon the same footing with other Articles furnished at that time and for that purpose." Lear's letter is recorded in the "Letter Book" in the *Washington Papers*.

On December 8, or thereabouts, Washington wrote out a memorandum of extracts from the report of the Commissioners appointed to treat with the southern Indians, and extracts of the letters from sundry persons in Kentucky and other parts of the western country, for the purpose of clarifying the Indian situation in his mind. This document, covering 18 folio pages, is in the *Washington Papers*.

[54] Not now found in the *Washington Papers*.

Senate have advised and consented to its ratification upon a condition which excepts part of one article. Agreeably thereto, and to the best judgment I was able to form of the public interest after full and mature deliberation, I have added my sanction. The result on the part of His Britannic Majesty is unknown. When received, the subject will without delay be placed before Congress.

This interesting summary of our affairs with regard to the foreign powers between whom and the United States controversies have subsisted, and with regard also to those of our Indian neighbors with whom we have been in a state of enmity or misunderstanding, opens a wide field for consoling and gratifying reflections. If by prudence and moderation on every side the extinguishment of all the causes of external discord which have heretofore menaced our tranquillity, on terms compatible with our national rights and honor, shall be the happy result, how firm and how precious a foundation will have been laid for accelerating, maturing, and establishing the prosperity of our country.

Contemplating the internal situation as well as the external relations of the United States, we discover equal cause for contentment and satisfaction. While many of the nations of Europe, with their American dependencies, have been involved in a contest unusually bloody, exhausting, and calamitous, in which the evils of foreign war have been aggravated by domestic convulsion and insurrection; in which many of the arts most useful to society have been exposed to discouragement and decay; in which scarcity of subsistence has imbittered other sufferings; while even the anticipations of a return of the blessings of peace and repose are alloyed by the sense of heavy and accumulating burthens, which press upon all the departments of industry and threaten to clog the future springs of government, our favored country, happy in a striking contrast, has enjoyed tranquillity - a tranquillity the more satisfactory because maintained at the expense of no duty. Faithful to ourselves, we have violated no obligation to others.

Our agriculture, commerce, and manufactures prosper beyond former example, the molestations of our trade (to prevent a continuance of which, however, very pointed remonstrances have been made) being overbalanced by the aggregate benefits which it derives from a neutral position. Our population advances with a celerity which, exceeding the most sanguine calculations, proportionally augments our strength and resources, and guarantees our future security.

Every part of the Union displays indications of rapid and various improvement; and with burthens so light as scarcely to be perceived, with resources fully adequate to our present exigencies, with governments founded on the genuine principles of rational liberty, and with mild and wholesome laws, is it too much to say that our country exhibits a spectacle of national happiness never surpassed, if ever before equaled?

Placed in a situation every way so auspicious, motives of commanding force impel us, with sincere acknowledgment to Heaven and pure love to our country, to unite our efforts to preserve, prolong, and improve our immense advantages. To cooperate with you in this desirable work is a fervent and favorite wish of my heart.

It is a valuable ingredient in the general estimate of our welfare that the part of our country which was lately the scene of disorder and insurrection now enjoys the blessings of quiet and order. The misled have abandoned their errors, and pay the respect to our Constitution and laws which is due from good citizens to the public authorities of the society. These circumstances have induced me to pardon generally the offenders here referred to, and to extend forgiveness to those who had been adjudged to capital punishment. For though I shall always think it a sacred duty to exercise with firmness and energy the constitutional powers with which I am vested, yet it appears to me no less consistent with the public good than it is with my personal feelings to mingle in the operations of Government every degree of moderation and tenderness which the national justice, dignity, and safety may permit.

Senate have advised and consented to its ratification upon a condition which excepts part of one article. Agreeably thereto, and to the best judgment I was able to form of the public interest after full and mature deliberation, I have added my sanction. The result on the part of His Britannic Majesty is unknown. When received, the subject will without delay be placed before Congress.

This interesting summary of our affairs with regard to the foreign powers between whom and the United States controversies have subsisted, and with regard also to those of our Indian neighbors with whom we have been in a state of enmity or misunderstanding, opens a wide field for consoling and gratifying reflections. If by prudence and moderation on every side the extinguishment of all the causes of external discord which have heretofore menaced our tranquillity, on terms compatible with our national rights and honor, shall be the happy result, how firm and how precious a foundation will have been laid for accelerating, maturing, and establishing the prosperity of our country.

Contemplating the internal situation as well as the external relations of the United States, we discover equal cause for contentment and satisfaction. While many of the nations of Europe, with their American dependencies, have been involved in a contest unusually bloody, exhausting, and calamitous, in which the evils of foreign war have been aggravated by domestic convulsion and insurrection; in which many of the arts most useful to society have been exposed to discouragement and decay; in which scarcity of subsistence has imbittered other sufferings; while even the anticipations of a return of the blessings of peace and repose are alloyed by the sense of heavy and accumulating burthens, which press upon all the departments of industry and threaten to clog the future springs of government, our favored country, happy in a striking contrast, has enjoyed tranquillity - a tranquillity the more satisfactory because maintained at the expense of no duty. Faithful to ourselves, we have violated no obligation to others.

Our agriculture, commerce, and manufactures prosper beyond former example, the molestations of our trade (to prevent a continuance of which, however, very pointed remonstrances have been made) being overbalanced by the aggregate benefits which it derives from a neutral position. Our population advances with a celerity which, exceeding the most sanguine calculations, proportionally augments our strength and resources, and guarantees our future security.

Every part of the Union displays indications of rapid and various improvement; and with burthens so light as scarcely to be perceived, with resources fully adequate to our present exigencies, with governments founded on the genuine principles of rational liberty, and with mild and wholesome laws, is it too much to say that our country exhibits a spectacle of national happiness never surpassed, if ever before equaled?

Placed in a situation every way so auspicious, motives of commanding force impel us, with sincere acknowledgment to Heaven and pure love to our country, to unite our efforts to preserve, prolong, and improve our immense advantages. To cooperate with you in this desirable work is a fervent and favorite wish of my heart.

It is a valuable ingredient in the general estimate of our welfare that the part of our country which was lately the scene of disorder and insurrection now enjoys the blessings of quiet and order. The misled have abandoned their errors, and pay the respect to our Constitution and laws which is due from good citizens to the public authorities of the society. These circumstances have induced me to pardon generally the offenders here referred to, and to extend forgiveness to those who had been adjudged to capital punishment. For though I shall always think it a sacred duty to exercise with firmness and energy the constitutional powers with which I am vested, yet it appears to me no less consistent with the public good than it is with my personal feelings to mingle in the operations of Government every degree of moderation and tenderness which the national justice, dignity, and safety may permit.

Gentlemen: Among the objects which will claim your attention in the course of the session, a review of our military establishment is not the least important. It is called for by the events which have changed, and may be expected still further to change, the relative situation of our frontiers. In this review you will doubtless allow due weight to the considerations that the questions between us and certain foreign powers are not yet finally adjusted, that the war in Europe is not yet terminated, and that our Western posts, when recovered, will demand provision for garrisoning and securing them. A statement of our present military force will be laid before you by the Department of War.

With the review of our Army establishment is naturally connected that of the militia. It will merit inquiry what imperfections in the existing plan further experience may have unfolded. The subject is of so much moment in my estimation as to excite a constant solicitude that the consideration of it may be renewed until the greatest attainable perfection shall be accomplished. Time is wearing away some advantages for forwarding the object, while none better deserves the persevering attention of the public councils.

While we indulge the satisfaction which the actual condition of our Western borders so well authorizes, it is necessary that we should not lose sight of an important truth which continually receives new confirmations, namely, that the provisions heretofore made with a view to the protection of the Indians from the violences of the lawless part of our frontier inhabitants are insufficient. It is demonstrated that these violences can now be perpetrated with impunity, and it can need no argument to prove that unless the murdering of Indians can be restrained by bringing the murderers to condign punishment, all the exertions of the Government to prevent destructive retaliations by the Indians will prove fruitless and all our present agreeable prospects illusory. The frequent destruction of innocent women and children, who are chiefly the victims of retaliation, must continue to shock humanity, and an enormous expense to drain the Treasury of the Union.

To enforce upon the Indians the observance of justice it is indispensable that there shall be competent means of rendering justice to them. If these means can be devised by the wisdom of Congress, and especially if there can be added an adequate provision for supplying the necessities of the Indians on reasonable terms (a measure the mention of which I the more readily repeat, as in all the conferences with them they urge it with solicitude), I should not hesitate to entertain a strong hope of rendering our tranquillity permanent. I add with pleasure that the probability even of their civilization is not diminished by the experiments which have been thus far made under the auspices of Government. The accomplishment of this work, if practicable, will reflect undecaying luster on our national character and administer the most grateful consolations that virtuous minds can know.

ACTS AND RESOLVES

OF

MASSACHUSETTS.

1788-89.

[Published by the Secretary of the Commonwealth, under authority of Chapter 104, Resolves of 1889.]

1787.— CHAPTER 55.

answered, are hereby empowered to issue their order to the master of such house of correction to discharge the said person from his or her said confinement, the charge arising therefrom being first paid in manner as is herein before provided, & the said master is hereby required to discharge him or her accordingly.

No African or negro, not a citizen of one of the United States shall be suffered to tarry within this Commonwealth.

Be it further Enacted by the authority aforesaid, that no person being an African or Negroe, other than a subject of the Emperor of *Morocco*, or a citizen of some one of the United States; to be evidenced by a certificate from the Secretary of the State of which he shall be a citizen, shall tarry within this Commonwealth, for a longer time than two months, & upon complaint made to any Justice of the Peace within this Commonwealth, that any such person has been within the same more than two months, the said Justice shall order the said person to depart out of this Commonwealth, & in case that the said African or Negroe shall not depart as aforesaid, any Justice of the Peace within this Commonwealth, upon complaint & proof made that such person has continued within this Commonwealth ten days after notice given him or her to depart as aforesaid, shall commit the said person to any house of correction within the County, there to be kept to hard labour agreeably to the rules & orders of the said house, until the sessions of the peace, next to be holden within & for the said County; and the master of the said house of correction is hereby required & directed to transmit an attested copy of the warrant of commitment to the said Court, on the first day of their said Session, & if upon trial at the said Court, it shall be made to appear that the said person has thus continued within the Commonwealth contrary to the tenor of this Act, he or she shall be whipped not exceeding ten stripes, and ordered to depart out of this Commonwealth within ten days; and if he or she shall not so depart, the same process shall be had and punishment inflicted, and so *toties quoties*.

March 26, 1788.

1787.— Chapter 55.

[February Session, ch. 23.]

Chap. 55. AN ACT FOR DIVIDING THE COUNTY OF *LINCOLN*, INTO THREE DISTRICTS, AND FOR ESTABLISHING A REGISTRY OF DEEDS AND COURT OF PROBATE, IN THE MIDDLE DISTRICT.

Preamble. Whereas the inhabitants of that part of the County of Lincoln, *which borders upon* Penobscot River, *and extend*

1790, which being agreed to, the following Message was accordingly prepared Vizt.

In the House of Representatives January 20th 1790

Honorable Gentlemen

This House propose to ratify such Acts and Ordinances as are engrossed, and the Great Seal of the State affixed thereto at 1 o'Clock this day, and then to Adjourn to Saturday the Twenty Seventh day of November next, to which this House request Your Honors Concurrence.

Ordered That the Message be signed by the Speaker, and that it be sent to the Senate and that Colonel Lushington and Mr. Drury Robertson do carry the same.

A petition was presented to the House from Sundry Free Moors, Subjects of the Emperor of Morocco; and residents in this State, praying that in case they should Commit Any Fault amenable to be brought to Justice, that they as Subjects to a Prince in Alliance with the United States of America, may be tried under the same Laws as the Citizens of this State would be liable to be tried, and not under the Negro Act, which was received and read.

[The humble Petition of Francis, Daniel, Hammond and Samuel, (Free Moors) in behalf of themselves and their wives Fatima, Flora, Sarah and

(page) 364 House Journal 4 January 1790- 20 January 1790

Clarinda, Humbly Sheweth That your Petitioners some years past had the misfortune while fighting in the defence of their Country, to be captured with their wives and made prisoners of War by one of the Kings of Africa. That a certain Captain Clark had them delivered to him on a promise that they should be redeemed by the Emperor of Morocco's Ambassador then residing in England, in order to have them returned to their own Country: *Instead of which* he brought them to this State, and sold them for slaves. Since that period they have by the greatest industry been enabled to purchase their freedom from their respective Masters: And now prayeth your Honorable House, That as free born subjects of a Prince now in Alliance with these United States; that they may not be considered as subject to a Law of this State (now in force) called the negro law: but if they should unfortunately be guilty of any crime or misdemeanor against the Laws of the Land, that they may have a just trial by a Lawful Jury. And your Petitioners as in duty bound will ever pray.][1]

Ordered That it be referred to a Committee, the following Gentlemen were accordingly appointed, Mr. Justice Grimke, General Pinckney & Mr. Edward Rutledge.

A petition was presented to the House from Sundry Inhabitants of Ninety Six District, praying that another Inspector of Tobacco for the Inspections at Campbells, Falmouth, and Adam's ferry Warehouses might be appointed, which was received and read.

Ordered That General Pinckney have leave to bring in An Ordinance agreeably to the prayer of the petitioners.

Major Pinckney from the Committee appointed to examine such Acts and Ordinances as are engrossed, and to get the great Seal of the State affixed thereto, Reported that there were Four Acts and Eight Ordinances ready for Ratifying.[2]

these former Moors and that in accordance with the fullest right of religious independence guaranteed every citizen we recognize also the right of these people to use the name affixes El or Ali or Bey or any other prefix or suffix to which they have heretofore been accustomed to use or which they may hereafter acquire the right to use.

On the question, Will the House Adopt the resolution? It was Adopted May 4, 1933

these former Moors and that in accordance with the fullest right of religious independence guaranteed every citizen we recognize also the right of these people to use the name affixes El or Ali or Bey or any other prefix or suffix to which they have heretofore been accustomed to use or which they may hereafter acquire the right to use.

On the question, Will the House Adopt the resolution? It was Adopted May 4, 1933

THE UNHOLY DAYS WE CELBRATE
WHERE DO THEY COME FROM?

Thanksgiving is said to be a day we celebrate as a result of the pilgrims who landed on Plymouth Rock giving thanks to the Indians who shared their bounty as well as taught the pilgrims how to farm, cultivate, and hunt. In commemoration of this generosity, we slaughter thousands of turkeys, add sides and feast. WRONG. This slaughtering of thousands of turkeys/ Turks did happen, but they were not birds. Case in point, the massacre at Wounded Knee.

Miniconjou Sioux Chief Big Foot lies dead in the snow of Wounded Knee, South Dakota, opposite. He was among the first to die in the fusillade that exploded on December 28, 1890, when fearful Miniconjous refused to surrender their weapons to some 500 artillery-equipped troops ordered to disarm them. Above, a mounted officer surveys the field three days after the one-sided battle. Civilian grave diggers bury the Miniconjou dead in a mass grave hacked from the frozen earth, left.

THE UNHOLY DAYS WE CELBRATE
WHERE DO THEY COME FROM?

After Thanksgiving, Americans celebrate Christmas; the mass for Christ. This one is centered around the conquering of the Moors. To comprehend this one, we need to comprehend the symbolism of this unholy day.

1. The major colors are red and green.
2. The pine tree.
3. The major ornament, the pentagram star.
4. The giving of gifts was the result of a Moorish warrior lost in battle and the Amir having gifts bestowed upon the warrior's wife and children.

BLACK INDIANS/ MOORS

Black Indians: Another fiction used to displace a people of their true identity. If we just learn to comprehend why a people have been relabeled every generation for the past 100 years, we would re-discover our true identity. African, Black Indians, Indians (outside of India), Negro, Nigger, Colored, black man, black American, black African, and African American.

What's next???

The names just mentioned have absolutely nothing to do with a people of a nation of people other than the fact that they were created to displace a people or a nation of people from the family of nations and cause them to be subjugated and relegated to the status of animal and chattel property.

From the Book of Genesis, it says God gave man the dominion over all the animals of the Earth.

In the words of the great Prophet, Noble Drew Ali, the Citizen of all free National Constitutions are all one family bearing one free National name. Those who fail to recognize the free National name of their Constitutional Government are classed as undesirables and are subjected to all inferior names, abuses and mistreatments that the citizens care to bestow upon them and it is a sin for a group of people to violate the national Constitutional Laws of a free National Government and cling to the names and principals that delude to slavery.

Omari Miles El

Delaware's Forgotten Folk

THE STORY OF THE MOORS & NANTICOKES

By
C. A. WESLAGER

With photographs by
L. T. Alexander

and drawings by
John Swientochowski

**BLACK RESOURCE CENTER
DO NOT CIRCULATE
IN-HOUSE USE ONLY**

UNIVERSITY OF PENNSYLVANIA PRESS
Philadelphia
1943

C. 53010

blacks and wanted to exist as such. A 1797 reference (see chap. 3 above) stated that of all the northern Indian tribes the Nanticokes were darkest in color, and this hereditary skin color among many of the descendants caused misunderstandings among uninformed whites, who had erroneously been taught that Indians had red skins.

Prior to the outbreak of the Civil War, Levin Sockum was one of the most prominent and prosperous Nanticokes living in Indian River Hundred. The name Sockum, which may have been derived from the Algonkian word *sakima*, meaning a chief (sometimes spelled *sackem*), was an old one among the Indians. In a journal written during a trip to western Pennsylvania in 1758, the Moravian Christian Frederick Post noted, "At fort Loudon we met about sixteen of the Cherokees, who came in a friendly manner to our Indians [Delawares], enquiring for Bill Sockum...." Fort Loudon was about a mile south of the present village of Fort Loudon in Franklin County, Pennsylvania, and was built in 1756. It was garrisoned by Provincial troops who joined General Forbes' forces, and many friendly Indians often congregated there.

Many years later an oldtime resident of Delaware's Nanticoke Indian community named Lemuel Sockum said that his ancestors were Cherokees." It would be difficult to argue this point, but Indian tradition in the Sockum family was certainly emphatic and consistent. Jim Sockum, one of Levin's sons, evidently returned to Delaware. Some of my elderly informants forty years ago still remembered him when they were youngsters and he was an old man. He wore his hair long and was as Indian in his facial features as a western Sioux, except that he wore a long beard. Sockum was a wanderer. He was reputed to have made sixteen trips on foot back and forth to Philadelphia, carrying an old gunny sack on his shoulder containing food. He slept in cemeteries, where he would not be molested by whites." One of the reasons he gave for the Philadelphia trips was to obtain treatment for his game leg, bitten by Dave Wright's horse, but this was probably just a rationalization for his trips. A story is told that on one of his journeys a watchdog came growling after him when he reached the edge of the city. He made friends with the dog and slipped off its collar. He then sold the collar for 25¢ to buy his breakfast.

Levin Sockum was a much more conventional person than his son and had a good sense of business. Evidently it was his success as a storekeeper that aroused the jealousy of white neighbors and in a spite suit that was tried in the court at Georgetown, I was told by members of the tribe, now deceased, that a white landowner named Nathaniel Burton instituted the suit. I have not been able to corroborate this because the indictment slips for 1855 are missing from the Georgetown court records. It is

Nanticokes Seek Recognition in Delaware

Sockum's independence, his moderate prosperity, and his insistence that he was an Indian.

What occurred was that in the course of his normal business Levin Sockum sold a quarter-pound of ammunition and a pound of shot to one of his Nanticoke neighbors, Isaiah Harmon. There was nothing irregular about the transaction because Sockum normally sold gunpowder, shot, and other commodities to his Indian customers.

At that time there was a statute on the law books in the state of Delaware that read:

If any person shall sell or loan any firearms to any negro or mulatto, he shall be deemed guilty of a misdemeanor, and shall be fined twenty dollars.

This law had been passed in the emotional stress following the 1831 rebellion of black slaves in Virginia incited by Nat Turner. The fear of an uprising of blacks resulted in the passage of legislature in Delaware prohibiting Negroes from using firearms, forbidding them to assemble after 10 P.M., and imposing other restrictions. The law pertaining to the sale of ammunition to blacks was amended in 1851 and again in 1852, and the latter act was invoked in the Sockum case.

Delaware's new attorney general, George P. Fisher, found it his duty to prosecute Sockum. Had Sockum sold ammunition to a Negro or mulatto? There was no question whether or not a sale was made, since both Sockum and Harmon admitted to the transaction. The legal issue in the case was whether Sockum's customer was an Indian, a Negro, a white, or a mulatto. Fisher later wrote in a newspaper article that Harmon was a fair, hazel-eyed young man twenty-five years old, with perfect Caucasian features, dark chestnut hair, rosy cheeks, and "the handsomest man in the court room, and yet he was alleged to be a mulatto."

Despite Fisher's own admission that Harmon had no Negro features, he set about to prove that Harmon was, in fact, a mulatto. Since this was one of Fisher's early cases as Delaware's attorney general, his reputation would not be enhanced if he lost the case, and he was determined to win even if it meant holding Harmon and Sockum up to shame and ridicule.

Fisher based his case on alleged genetic evidence, completely ignoring the fact that Indian identity is a phenomenon of the social relations in a mixed-blood community, rather than basic physical differences among the individual members of the community. Fair complexion and hazel eyes by no means negate an Indian cultural heritage in such groups. For instance, many Houma Indian descendants in southern Louisiana, who freely admit to strong white admixture, cannot be distinguished by phenotype from

LENAPE HISTORY

MUNSEE AND DELAWARE (LENNI LENAPE) PEOPLE

The Delaware and Munsee or Minisink (Mahican)Indians are an ancient group from the Agonquian language speaking group of Native Americans who covered a large part of Central and Eastern North America. Our origin is very old and could go back, according to recent discoveries, as far as 30,000 years or more. We called ourselves "*Lenni Lanape*"; of which the origin of these words are very old. They are said to mean: "*original man*", "*first man*", "*ancient man*", or "*true or common man*". The term "*Delaware*"; is said to have come from more of where we were than **who** we were. It is believed that we got the name from the river named after Thomas West, Baron De La War, who was the Colony of Virginia's first governor. After a period of time the name came to be given to all of the indians living long the river in the early 1600.

At the time of the arrival of the Europeans, the Lenape probably numbered between 16,000 to 20,000 people and lived from as far north as central New York to as far south as southern Maryland and at times Virginia. Inland as far as central Pennsylvania and Maryland. **Before** the Euros, from a period of time between 1000ad and the late 1300's to early 1400's, we may have lived in Ohio and western Pennsylvania. It is believed by some, that in the 1300's we may have forced the descendants of the mound builders in Ohio, the Cherokees, out of Ohio and south into Kentucky and Tennessee only to assist them a century later with the Shawnee (sister tribe to the Delaware) in there battle with the Catatwa, related or ancestor of the Lakota people who later became the plains indians. The Shawnee at that time lived in northern Georgia at this time.

Most of the time in history, the various bands, tribes, and villages, even though they had a shared culture, seldom were led by a singe head or council until dealing with the governments made it a necessity to unite from time to time for their survival to do so.

Social events and ceremonies were a different matter and on various times in the year they would get together to share food and spiritual traditions.

The Lenape are divided into three main tribes or bands and each tribe had three primary "*clans*". The clans are the Wolf, Turtle, and the Turkey clans. Until the late 1700's, there was also a "*Crow or Raven*" clan. Its job was to prepare the dead. There is little known of this clan other then it is said that they were at the bottom of the social scale.

The three tribes were the Minsi (Munsee/Mahican); which meant "*Stone Land or Mountain People*", believed by scientist to be the oldest tribe as well as the tribe that stayed pretty much in the mountains of Pennsylvania and New York since about 1000ad. The Munsee were the primary meat gatherers of the Delaware as farming was very difficult in the mountains rocky soil. The Delaware referred to the Munsee as the "*Wolf Tribe*".

The next tribe of the Delaware were the "*Unamis or Turtle Tribe*". The largest of the three tribes; it did the majority of the farming as they lived in the valleys and along the river in the Delaware Bay areas inland to the Susquehanna Rivers.

The last tribe is the "*Unalachticos or Turkey Tribe*" who lived on the sea coast of primarily New Jersey and did the majority of fishing, oystering, and other type of shell fishing. How long they were known by that name is up for debate as the first time in print that they were referred to was in the late 1700's at a meeting at Fort Pitt (Pittsburgh). In ancient times there were probably at least eight other clans or tribes that made up Lanape as well as many as 20 subtribes such as the Shanticoke, Nanticoke, Manhattens, Mohicans and many, many, more tribes.

Over the next 300 hundred years, the Lenape were forced to move west by a series of treaties that saw the Lenape's land holdings dwindle away. The tribe in the late 1700's had already had been moved out of Pennsylvania and into Ohio as early as 1715 with the bulk of them moving into Ohio after 1750. Some bands of the Munsee (the Stockbridge Munsee) had moved to the what was to become the state of Wisconsin as early as the late 1600's to early 1700's by early missionaries who were well aware that the Lenape were being forced out and that the white man, with his never ending quest for land westward eventually would force them out of Pennsylvania and so hoped by moving to Wisconsin their culture would be spared. This did by them some time and they are still there and are one of the few tribes of Lenape that hasn't had to move over the last three centuries. The rest were not so lucky.

The greatest loss of land came with the signing of the Greenville Treaty of 1795 in which all of the indians of the Ohio Valley would be required to give up nearly 2/3 of their land holdings in exchange for pennies on the dollars for what it was worth. The Delaware and Shawnees, along with Miamis, Wyandotte, and other tribes of the area were to move, first to Indiana and then to Missouri by 1820's and eventually to Kansas by 1836. The *"Treaty of St. Mary"* on October 3, 1818 ceded the remaining land in Ohio, which roughly followed north of present day U.S. Route 36 and State Routes 39, 540, and 541 was held near the present day town of Wapakoneta, Ohio. Only a small part of land north of there remained and it too was annexed to Ohio in 1836. By 1840, most but not all of the Delaware had left their Ohio homeland. Those that remained had often married non native wives and husbands and were considered *"civilized"* and left alone. Others, such as Chief Beaver's band eventually moved as far as Texas but were soon made to moved back to *"Indian Territory"* (Oklahoma) in 1877. just as with the *"Indian Removal Act of 1830"*, which dictated that all indians be removed to west of the Mississippi River a similar act past in the 1870's forced the Texas band back to Oklahoma. Those that remained in Ohio are what made up the **Munsee Thames River Delaware Indian Nation-USA** now known as the **Munsee Delaware Indian Nation-USA**. These remnants, some which returned to Ohio after the last treaty with the Delaware in 1866 which gave the Delawares the choice to elect to dissolve their relations with their tribe and join the Cherokees as U.S. citizens in Oklahoma and give up by forced sale of their lands in Kansas. Most agreed to this but some refused. Some of these descendants still live in Kansas and today are known as the Kansas Delaware. Others such as the **Munsee Delaware Indian Nation-USA** either never left Ohio or some of those families came back to Ohio and joined there friends and relatives with the Ohio Band. Today, the Munsee and Delawares, are scattered from the west coast to the east coast. The Federal Delawares, those who moved to Oklahoma, are known today as *"The Delaware Tribe of Oklahoma"*, the eastern Oklahoma Delawares, and the *"Absentees"* of western Oklahoma. There are three Canadian tribes, Munsee Delaware of the Thames, near Thamesville, Ontario Canada, Morraviantown Delaware, who got their name from the Morravian priests who moved them there in the late 1700's and the six nations reservation group that live on the Iroquois reservation north of New York. Other bands of the Delaware, such as the *"Kansas Delaware"* in Kansas, the *"Idaho Delaware"*, and in the east **The Munsee Delaware Indian Nation-USA**, and its sub tribes, *"The Eastern Lenape Nation"*, mainly in the Pennsylvania area east, and *"The United Lenape Band"* to the south, the latter with a large Cherokee population as well.

There are other Delaware tribes as well in Pennsylvania and New York (Delaware Indian Nation-PA). And in New Jersey, a very old tribe, the *"Sand Hill"* tribe. In this past decade, the last of the full blood Delaware have died. Like the dinosaur, the Lenape are nearly extinct; leaving only a few to carry on the traditions from a time long ago when the earth was pure, as well as the air and water. The Lenape have always been known as *"The Keepers of the Earth"* and will continue this path and seekers of peace has always been our way. Honor those <u>few</u> that have chosen this path, for as long as their is <u>one</u> Lenape left our rich heritage will survive...

For more info on the Lenape, we suggest the following:

The Lenape
Robert S. Grumet - Indians of North America 1989

Dikon Among the Lenape, the New Jersey Delaware
Harrigton - 1937

The Lenape and their Legends
Daniel G. Briton - 1884

The Lenape, Archaeology, History, and Ethnography
Herbert C. Kraft - 1986

For more info-language and clothing:

Western Delaware Tribe of Oklahoma web page at www.westerndelaware.nsn.us.

Lehigh County (Allentown, Pennsylvania) Historical Society's web page at www.lenape.org.

Shawnee (Ohio) web page at www.zaneshawneecaverns.org.

Delaware Tribe of Indians web page at www.delawaretribeofindians.nsn.us.

Lenape Delaware History Web Site at http://lenape-delawarehistory.freeyellow.com

MUNSEE INDIANS, an American tribe of the Delaware family, originally one of the three great divisions of that race. They were sometimes called the Wolf tribe of the Delawares. They resided along the Delaware River, and in New York, Pennsylvania and New Jersey. During the Revolution many of the Munsees removed to Canada, where at Thames, Ontario, there are some survivors. At Green Bay, Wis., is another tribal remnant and a third remnant is found in Kansas; in all, less than 100 in the United States. See Delaware Indians.

"Munsee Indians". *Encyclopedia Americana.* 1920.

MUNSEES, Monseys, or Minsis, a tribe of American Indians formerly residing on the upper Delaware and the Minisink. In 1663 they aided the Esopus Indians in attacking the Dutch post, and were chastised by Kregier. They claimed all the land from the Minisink to the Hudson, the head waters of the Delaware and Susquehanna, and south to the Lehigh and Conewago. Settlers began to encroach on them early in the 18th century, and they fell back to the Susquehanna. The Moravians drew some to their missions, but the main body were discontented; moving westward through the Iroquois country, they joined the French at Niagara, and were with difficulty gained over by Sir William Johnson. After the fall of the French, some listened to the Moravians, but in the revolution most of the tribe, under Capt. Pipe, retired to Sandusky and joined the English, and even after the war remained hostile, rejecting terms in 1793, and not making peace till 1805. In 1808 a part settled on Miami land at White river. Some years later they joined the Stockbridge Indians near Green bay. Most of the Munsees, under a treaty in 1839, removed to Kansas. They are now nearly extinct, being represented in Wisconsin by a single family of half a dozen souls, and in Kansas by part of a band of 56 Chippewas and Munsees. Their language was an Algonquin dialect closely allied to the Delaware.

"Munsees". *The American Cyclopædia.* 1879.

MUN'SEE. A subtribe of the Delaware (q.v.), originally constituting one of the three great divisions of that tribe and dwelling along the upper streams of the Delaware River, and the adjacent country in New York, New Jersey, and Pennsylvania. They were considered the most warlike portion of the tribe and assumed the leadership in war councils. From their principal totem they were frequently called the Wolf tribe of the Delaware. They were prominent in the early history of New York and New Jersey, being among the first tribes of that region to meet the whites. By a noted fraudulent treaty known as the Walking Purchase, the main body was forced to remove from the Delaware River about the year 1740. They settled on the Susquehanna, on lands assigned them by the Iroquois, but soon afterwards moved westward and joined the main Delaware tribe on the Ohio River, with whom the greater portion eventually became incorporated. A considerable body, who were converted by the Moravian missionaries, drew off from the rest and formed a separate organization, most of them removing to Canada during the Revolution. Others joined the Ojibwa and Stockbridge Indians. The majority were incorporated in the Delaware, with whom they participated in their subsequent wars and removals. Those who still keep the name of Munsee are in three bands, two of which are consolidated with other tribal fragments, so that no separate census is available. These tribes are the Munsee of the Thames, Ontario, Canada, 120; Munsee (or Christian), and Chippewa, northeastern Kansas, 90; and Stockbridge and Munsee, Green Bay Agency, Wis., 530. Those of the United States are officially reported as civilized and entirely competent to manage their own affairs. The mixed band in Kansas has dissolved tribal relations.

The New International Encyclopedia "Munsee" Edited by Daniel Coit Gilman, Harry Thurston Peck and Frank Moore Colby (1905)

The Delaware natives, also called the Lenape, originally lived along the Delaware River in New Jersey. They speak a form of the Algonquian language and are thus related to the Miami natives, Ottawa natives, and Shawnee natives. The Delawares were called "Grandfathers" by the other Algonquian tribes because of their belief that the Delawares were among the oldest groups in the Algonquian nation.

As British colonists immigrated to North America, the Delawares fled westward away from the land-hungry Europeans. While trying to escape the British colonists, the Delawares encountered the Iroquois natives, who struggled with the Delawares and drove them further west. Some Delaware natives came to live in eastern Ohio along the Muskingum River, while others resided in northwestern Ohio along the Auglaize River. Once in Ohio, the Delawares grew into a powerful tribe that often resisted the further advances of the Iroquois.

Upon arriving in the Ohio Country, the Delawares formed alliances with Frenchmen engaged in the fur trade. The French provided the natives with European cookware and guns, as well as alcohol, in return for furs. This alliance would prove to be temporary at best, as French and British colonists struggled for control of the Ohio Country beginning in the 1740s. As one European power gained control of the area the Delawares chose to ally themselves with the stronger party. This was the case until the Treaty of Paris (1763) ended the French and Indian War. As a result of this war, the French abandoned all of their North American colonies to Britain. The Delawares thereafter remained loyal to the British and the American colonists until the American Revolution.

During the Revolution, the Delawares became a divided people. Many attempted to remain neutral in the conflict, especially those who had adopted Christianity and lived in Moravian Church missions at Schoenbrunn and Gnadenhutten in what is now eastern Ohio. Other Delawares supported the British, who had replaced the French traders at the end of the French and Indian War. These natives thanked Britain for the Proclamation of 1763, which prohibited colonists from settling any further west than the Appalachian Mountains. They feared that if the Americans were victorious, the Delawares would be driven from their lands. Despite the Delawares' fears, many Americans hoped that they could count on the tribe as allies. As the war progressed, however, not all Americans trusted them. In 1782, a group of Pennsylvania militiamen, falsely believing the natives were responsible for several raids, killed almost one hundred Christian Delawares in what became known as the Gnadenhutten Massacre. Although these Delawares were friendly to the Americans, they suffered due to the fears of some of their white neighbors.

Following the American victory in the Revolution, the Delawares struggled against whites as they moved onto the natives' territory. In 1794, General Anthony Wayne defeated the Delawares and other Ohio natives at the Battle of Fallen Timbers. The natives surrendered most of their Ohio lands with the signing of the Treaty of Greeneville in 1795.

In 1829, the United States forced the Delawares to relinquish their remaining land in Ohio and move west of the Mississippi River.

"Delaware Indians" http://www.ohiohistorycentral.org/w/Delaware_Indians

---

The Munsee natives were part of the Delaware natives, although they lived separately from the Delaware nation for most of their existence. Some scholars argue that the Munsee natives should not be considered Delaware because of some stark differences in dialect. The United States referred to the Munsees as a separate tribe in the Treaty of Fort Industry. The Munsee natives were Algonquian natives. The Algonquian natives consisted of various tribes that spoke similar languages. The Munsees lived originally in New York and New Jersey, but they moved westward as whites forced them from the land. By the 1720s, the Munsee natives had reached western Pennsylvania. There, missionaries from the Moravian Church attained some success in converting the Munsees to Christianity.

http://www.ohiohistorycentral.org/w/Munsee_Indians?rec=613

This antique French print preserves some Black Indians found in Spanish California before the U.S. arrival.

In the 1790s he sold it and became mayor of Los Angeles. The governor of California before the arrival of the U.S. armed forced was Pio Pico. Governor Pico came from a prominent California family with African ancestors.

The arrival of U.S. rule changed life in California. Under Spain and Mexico about 15 percent of Californians had listed themselves as African in heritage. This population disappeared on U.S. Census rolls. Slavery, racial animosity, and California's new "Black Laws" drove them across to the safe side of the invisible color line.

Little is known about the Black Indians who strode or rode across California's trails after that. One white pioneer remembered a black man preaching to Native Americans in their own language near the Canadian River. He also reported that on the Santa Fe trail black people "have a great deal of influence with the Indians." At Fort Kearny he found a black interpreter using his knowledge of Spanish and Indian languages to provide U.S. authorities with valuable information.

Entitled "America," this antique French engraving shows African and Native American people living in harmony and happiness in their own village.

Some colonies were begun by a single African or Indian, and others were the result of several or many slaves fleeing together. The history of the Saramaka people of Surinam in South America started around 1685 when African and native slaves escaped and together formed a maroon society. For eight generations Dutch armed forces tried to crush their community, but today it is still alive and boasts twenty thousand members. For the Saramakans liberty came in 1761 when Europeans abandoned their wars and sued for peace.

Your Majesty, ... the time is coming when these [African] people will have become masters of the Indians, inasmuch as they were born among them and their maidens, and are men who dare to die as well as any Spaniard in the world. ... I do not know who will be in a position to resist them.

It was in Mexico that Europeans made their strongest effort to keep Africans apart from Native Americans. Black men far outnumbered their women and so sought Indian wives. A Native American wife meant, if she was free, that children born to her would be free, not slaves. So extensive,

This old French engraving of the Osage Indian Nation shows the variation in color types present in one Native American Nation. (Note how all faces have been "romanized" with straight noses.)

These Black Indians of southern Mexico used such primitive weapons as the bow and arrow to protect their families from modern European weaponry.

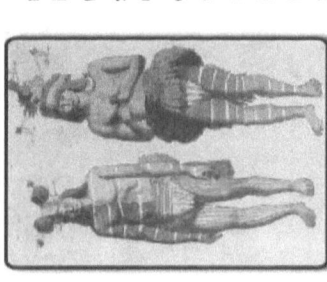

Three males and two females neophytes from mission San Francisco. Notice details of female tattoos and coiffeur styles. The somber countenances on these Costanoan Indians reflect the culture shock and stress of the mission's program to rapidly transform the hunting and collecting peoples into a disciplined labor force. French artist Louis Choris made this disturbing observation that is amply reflected in this 1822 lithograph: "I have never seen one smile, I have never seen one look one in the eye." (Courtesy The Bancroft Library, University of California, Berkeley)

Ohlone dancers dressed for a ceremonial dance.

A mixed group of mission San Francisco neophytes of Costanoan and Coast Miwok tribes as depicted in a Louis Choris lithograph in 1822. The woman with a garland in her hair is a member of the North Bay Coast Miwok Numpali. (Courtesy The Bancroft Library, University of California, Berkeley)

Opposite, below: Louis Choris, French artist on the 1816 Russian expedition of Lt. Otto Von Kotzebue's visit to Alta California, drew this ink and watercolor sketch of Costanoan Indians in the vicinity of mission San Francisco. The inscription reads: "*Costumes de danse de guerre des habitans de la California*." The body painting and elaborate flicker feather headdresses are typical of north central California ceremonial regalia. This, in fact, may not have been a war dance regalia. (Courtesy the Honeyman Collection, The Bancroft Library, University of California, Berkeley)

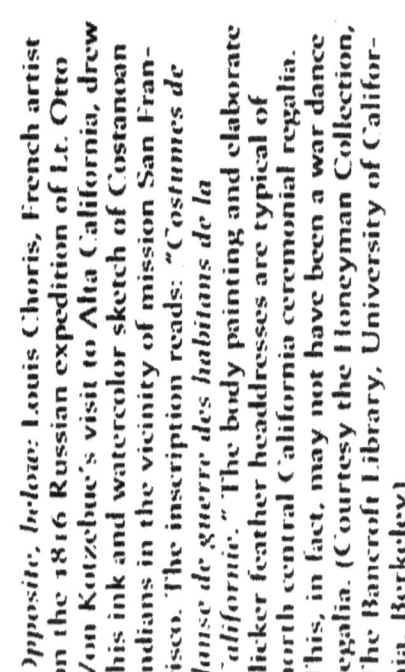

Negro Abraham WITH THE FLORIDA INDIANS

The purchase of Florida from Spain in 1819 came about as the indirect result of the fraternity which existed between red men and black men. Each year, hundreds of slaves valued by their owners at about $2,000 each, ran away from plantations in the Georgia territory and joined the Indians of Florida. On the excuse of punishing Indian marauders and hunting runaway slaves, the U.S. army invaded the Indian villages in the Spanish territories in 1817, and incited the First Seminole War. In treaties relocating the Creeks and Seminoles from Florida to Oklahoma and Kansas after the war, reference is made to "their faithful interpreter, Abraham."

Negro Abraham (Black Abraham) was a fugitive slave adopted by the Seminole Indians. Born in Pensacola, Florida, in the early 1800s, he escaped and sought shelter with the Seminoles in 1826. He learned the language and customs, and became known as "prophet", "principal counselor of his master, Chief Micanopy," and "high chancellor and keeper of the king's conscience." An American officer described him as having "the crouch and spring of a panther."

Although uneducated, he was a persuasive and eloquent speaker; "a perfect Talleyrand of the Savage Court of Florida," said one writer. As one of the spokesmen and interpreters for the Seminole nation, he at first opposed their relocation, not only because it was an injustice to the Indians but because he feared that, in traveling across the Southern states, many of the Negroes would be recaptured by the slave hunters.

Negro Abraham.

He also opposed mingling the Seminoles with the Creeks because the latter were known to enslave Negroes; and in the Fort Dade Treaty of 1837, demanded a guarantee against domination by the Creeks. In 1838, he finally helped convince the tribes to accept the U.S. demands for the sake of the women and children. Negotiating to secure the best terms possible, he agreed to investigate the proposed site in Oklahoma, and refused to the move until he was assured of everybody's freedom.

Wilhelmena Robinson, *Historical Negro Biographies* (New York: Publishers Co., 1967). Benjamin Brawley, *A Social History of the American Negro* (New York: Collier Books, 1970).

This antique French print preserves some Black Indians found in Spanish California before the U.S. arrival.

Using double-bladed paddles with pointed ends, two Coast Miwok Indians speed a passenger across San Francisco Bay in a fast, light canoe made of woven tule reeds in a tinted lithograph by Louis Choris. Another Choris lithograph (inset) depicts hunters of the Northern Valley Yokuts stalking game.

making similar strides farther north. In 1770 a second mission had been established a few hundred miles up the coast at Monterey, the site chosen as the capital of the new Spanish territory. Three more missions had since been founded between the first two, and another was in planning. The conversion of the native Californians seemed to be proceeding apace.

Soon after the feast of Saint Francis, however, a pair of influential neophytes named Zegotay and Francisco renounced their ties to Mission San Diego. When they failed to appear there for several days, the sergeant of the presidio and a group of soldiers went out to bring in the two "deserters," as the priests called them. Nothing could have been more provocative to the Kumeyaay. Father Jayme had warned his superiors of the ill will already stirred up by the presence of troops. At one nearby village, he said,

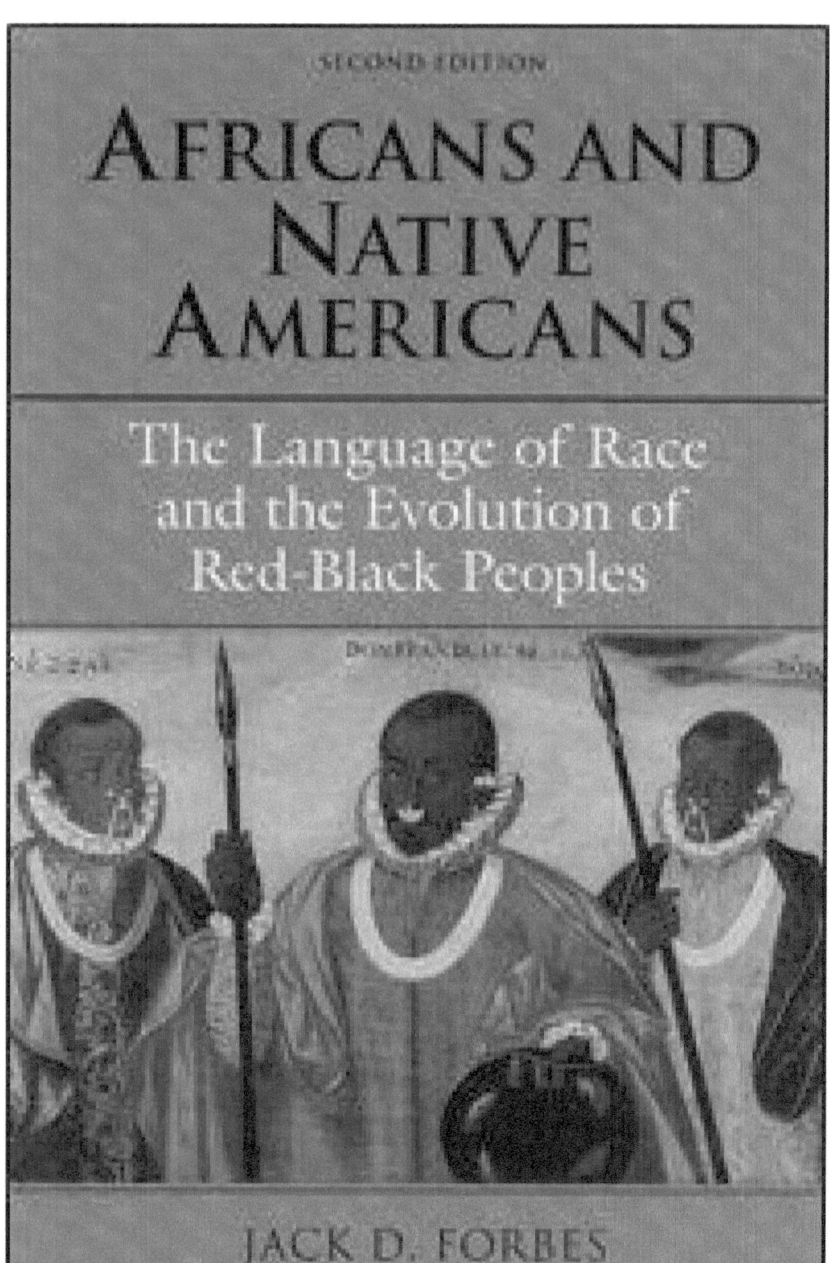

Seminole warriors of Florida evaded and punished United States troops, as opposite, in three conflicts from 1817 to 1858, wars that they won in the field but lost at the negotiating table. Effective guerrilla action was the Seminole specialty. Their leader, Osceola, was subsequently seized in violation of a truce, and died in prison only a few days after George Catlin had painted his portrait, left, in 1837. Escaped slaves found refuge with these southern Indians and often married into the tribe. Below, Black Seminoles appear in festive wedding dress.

with a code of laws, a court, and a bicameral legislature. A foreign visitor would have had difficulty distinguishing a Cherokee settlement from any number of rural white communities that were composed of well-tended farms, handsome plantations, and a slave-holding class of planters. Cherokee settlements even included a few Christians, who honored the Sabbath and read the New Testament (which had been translated into Cherokee).

The only flaw in this idyllic scene is that the Cherokees were Indians and the land they occupied was fertile and coveted by whites. Moreover, in 1802 the federal government had promised much of the Cherokee domain to the state of Georgia to resolve a dispute that had lingered since the American Revolution. The agreement called for the federal government to free Georgia of its Indian population "as soon as the same can be peaceably done on reasonable terms."

Under the able leadership of John Ross, the Cherokees used every weapon in the legal and political arsenal of the United States in an effort to save their eastern homelands. Despite the vigorous assistance of sympathetic Congressmen and the favorable decisions by Supreme Court Justice

Under armed guard, tribes of the Old South were all but herded west across the Mississippi River in the first half of the 19th century. Here, a group of Cherokees is depicted during a day's travel. Sixteen thousand Cherokees were moved during 1838 in what 19th-century historians called The Trail of Tears. As many as a quarter of the travelers may have died. While most tribes were removed from the East to Oklahoma's Indian Territory, some were marched there from the Far West or settled in areas often unsuited to occupations assigned to them by whites. A few bands rebelled, fleeing the reservations in generally hopeless bids for freedom; some crossed into Canada or Mexico.

1705 A Virginia slavery act decreed that all imported servants were to remain in lifelong servitude. Excepted were those who had been Christians in their native country or who had been free in a Christian country. This law limited slavery to blacks and confined almost all imported blacks to slavery. An interesting exception was inserted for "Turks and Moors in amity with her majesty."

My power of immunity is further substantiated by the Roman Catholic Magna Charta Civil Laws Code in Philadelphia, Pennsylvania in the year 1854. This governs only the rights and conduct of the "white" people, Christians and Jews of the 1363 Union States Rights Republic under the Magna Charta Knights of Columbus and Ku Klux Klan Oath: To never allow the descendants of the Moorish Nation of this hemisphere to ever become citizens of the Union States Republic · U.S.A.

This Seminole delegation to Washington, D.C., in 1825 included "Negro Abraham" (center rear) as interpreter and as representative of their large black minority.

Boley's Town Council ruled one of some twenty-five to twenty-seven all-black settlements built in Oklahoma from 1890 to 1910.

women, and children were carried off and sold in southern slave markets.

The position of Black Seminoles, once secure within the nation, now needed strong support from Seminole chiefs. Division entered villages as chiefs argued various courses of action that might leave them in peace. Some Seminole chiefs claimed they now "owned" their black members, since that was the only language whites understood. But some who claimed this ownership took advantage of it and sent their black villagers off to labor hard in their fields.

Seminole law making it impossible to sell a slave remained firmly in place. Seminole chiefs still married black women and had black military and diplomatic advisors. But U.S. policy had begun to erode a strong friendship and trust and to bend equality.

In the face of their changing relations some Black Seminoles left to form their own settlements, and in 1822 the U.S. Secretary of State reported that in Florida there were "five or six hundred maroon negroes wild in the woods." Further south on the peninsula there were even

Oklahoma. He organized his people in Langston for another land rush in September 1891. That day McCabe was fired on by three whites and only rescued by black citizens wielding Winchesters.

McCabe was later picked to serve in a minor state office, but left his job the day Oklahoma became a state in the Union. It was hardly the Oklahoma of opportunity he had envisioned.

Black residents tried mightily to prevent Oklahoma from becoming another segregationist southern state. They formed the Equal Rights Association, the Suffrage League, the Afro-American League, the Negro Protective League, and smaller local protest associations. Some flavor of their sentiments can be seen in the words of the Equal Rights Association of Kingfisher County meeting in convention in 1904:

BLACKS/ MOORS IN THE CONFEDERACY
FACTS ABOUT CONFEDERATE BLACKS

Black Confederate Fact Sheet [fwd]

- *To*: afrigeneas@MsState.Edu
- *Subject*: Black Confederate Fact Sheet [fwd]
- *From*: AfriArc@aol.com
- *Date*: Thu, 12 Feb 1998 07:32:59 -0600
- *Sender*: owner-afrigeneas@MsState.Edu

From: CMBarker
Hi, folks..

Here's some interesting stuff "Black Confederate fact sheet" from Scott Williams (swcelt@stlnet.com)

Mark

Since attachments give some people trouble, I am again posting my "Black Confederate Fact sheet" but this time in the body of the message. Please review this and let me know if there are any glaring errors. I plan to distribute this next month when all the Black Yankee adoration is in full force.

Scott Williams
Sterling Price Camp
St. Louis, MO

Black Confederates
Why haven't we heard more about them? National Park Service historian, Ed Bearrs, stated, "I don't want to call it a conspiracy to ignore the role of Blacks both above and below the Mason-Dixon line, but it was definitely a tendency that began around 1910" Historian, Erwin L. Jordan, Jr., calls it a "cover-up" which started back in 1865. He writes, "During my research, I came across instances where Black men stated they were soldiers, but you can plainly see where 'soldier' is crossed out and 'body servant' inserted, or 'teamster' on pension applications." Another black historian, Roland Young, says he is not surprised that blacks fought. He explains that "Some, if not most, Black southerners would support their country" and that by doing so they were "demonstrating it's possible to hate the system of slavery and love one's country." This is the very same reaction that most African Americans showed during the American Revolution, where they fought for the colonies, even though the British offered them freedom if they fought for them.

It has been estimated that over 65,000 Southern blacks were in the Confederate ranks. Over 13,000 of these, "saw the elephant" also known as meeting the enemy in combat. These Black Confederates included both slave and free. The Confederate Congress did not approve blacks to be officially enlisted as soldiers (except as musicians), until late in the war. But in the ranks it was a different story. Many Confederate officers did not obey the mandates of politicians, they frequently enlisted blacks with the simple criteria, "Will you fight?" Historian Ervin Jordan, explains that "biracial units" were frequently organized "by local Confederate and State militia Commanders in response to immediate threats in the form of Union raidsÖ". Dr. Leonard Haynes, a African-American professor at Southern University, stated, "When you eliminate the black Confederate soldier, you've eliminated the history of the South."

1. The "Richmond Howitzers" were partially manned by black militiamen. They saw action at 1st Manassas (or 1st Battle of Bull Run) where they operated battery no. 2. In addition two black "regiments", one free and one slave, participated in the battle on behalf of the South. "Many colored people were killed in the action", recorded John Parker, a former slave. Free black musicians, cooks, soldiers and teamsters earned the same pay as white confederate privates. This was not the case in the Union army where blacks did not receive equal pay.

2. At least one Black Confederate was a non-commissioned officer. James Washington, Co. D 34th Texas Cavalry, "Terrell's Texas Rangers" became it's 3rd Sergeant.

3. At the Confederate Buffalo Forge in Rockbridge County, Virginia, skilled black workers "earned on average three times the wages of white Confederate soldiers and more than most Confederate army officers ($350-$600 a year)!

4. Dr. Lewis Steiner, Chief Inspector of the United States Sanitary Commission while observing Gen. "Stonewall" Jackson's occupation of Frederick, Maryland, in 1862: "Over 3,000 Negroes must be included in this number [Confederate troops]. These were clad in all kinds of uniforms, not only in cast-off or captured United States uniforms, but in coats with Southern buttons, State buttons, etc. These were shabby, but not shabbier or seedier than those worn by white men in the rebel ranks. Most of the Negroes had arms, rifles, muskets, sabers, bowie-knives, dirks, etc.....and were manifestly an integral portion of the Southern Confederate Army."

5. Frederick Douglas reported, "There are at the present moment many Colored men in the Confederate Army doing duty not only as cooks, servants and laborers, but real soldiers, having musket on their shoulders, and bullets in their pockets, ready to shoot down any loyal troops and do all that soldiers may do to destroy the Federal government and build up that of theÖrebels."

6. Black and white militiamen returned heavy fire on Union troops at the Battle of Griswoldsville (near Macon, GA). Approximately 600 boys and elderly men were killed in this skirmish.

7. In 1864, President Jefferson Davis approved a plan that proposed the emancipation of slaves, in return for the official recognition of the Confederacy by Britain and France. France showed interest but Britain refused.

8. The Jackson Battalion included two companies of black soldiers. They saw combat at Petersburg under Col. Shipp. "My men acted with utmost promptness and goodwill...Allow me to state sir that they behaved in an extraordinary acceptable manner."

9. Recently the National Park Service, with a recent discovery, recognized that blacks were asked to help defend the city of Petersburg, Virginia and were offered their freedom if they did so. Regardless of their official classification, black Americans performed support functions that in today's army many would be classified as official military service. The successes of white Confederate troops in battle, could only have been achieved with the support these loyal black Southerners.

10. Confederate General John B. Gordon (Army of Northern Virginia) reported that all of his troops were in favor of Colored troops and that it's adoption would have "greatly encouraged the army". Gen. Lee was anxious to receive regiments of black soldiers. The Richmond Sentinel reported on 24 Mar 1864, "NoneÖwill deny that our servants are more worthy of respect than the motley hordes which come against us." "Bad faith [to black Confederates] must be avoided as an indelible dishonor."

11. In March 1865, Judah P. Benjamin, Confederate Secretary Of State, promised freedom for blacks who served from the State of Virginia. Authority for this was finally received from the State of Virginia and on April 1st 1865, $100 bounties were offered to black soldiers. Benjamin exclaimed, "Let us say to every Negro who wants to go into the ranks, go and fight, and you are freeÖFight for your masters and you shall have your freedom." Confederate Officers were ordered to treat them humanely and protect them from "injustice and oppression".

12. A quota was set for 300,000 black soldiers for the Confederate States Colored Troops. 83% of Richmond's male slave population volunteered for duty. A special ball was held in Richmond to raise money for uniforms for these men. Before Richmond fell, black Confederates in gray uniforms drilled in the streets. Due to the war ending, it is believed only companies or squads of these troops ever saw any action. Many more black soldiers fought for the North, but that difference was simply a difference because the North instituted this progressive policy more sooner than the more conservative South. Black soldiers from both sides received discrimination from whites who opposed the concept .

13. Union General U.S. Grant in Feb 1865, ordered the capture of "all the Negro menÖ before the enemy can put them in their ranks." Frederick Douglas warned Lincoln that unless slaves were guaranteed freedom (those in Union controlled areas were still slaves) and land bounties, "they would take up arms for the rebels".

14. On April 4, 1865 (Amelia County, VA), a Confederate supply train was exclusively manned and guarded by black Infantry. When attacked by Federal Cavalry, they stood their ground and fought off the charge, but on the second charge they were overwhelmed. These soldiers are believed to be from "Major Turner's" Confederate command.

15. A Black Confederate, George _____, when captured by Federals was bribed to desert to the 'other side. He defiantly spoke, "Sir, you want me to desert, and I ain't no deserter. Down South, deserters disgrace their families and I am never going to do that."

16. Former slave, Horace King, accumulated great wealth as a contractor to the Confederate Navy. He was also an expert engineer and became known as the "Bridge builder of the Confederacy." One of his bridges was burned in a Yankee raid. His home was pillaged by Union troops, as his wife pleaded for mercy.

17. As of Feb. 1865 1,150 black seamen served in the Confederate Navy. One of these was among the last Confederates to surrender, aboard the CSS Shenandoah, six months after the war ended. This surrender took place in England.

18. Nearly 180,000 Black Southerners, from Virginia alone, provided logistical support for the Confederate military. Many were highly skilled workers. These included a wide range of jobs: nurses, military engineers, teamsters, ordnance department workers, brakemen, firemen, harness makers, blacksmiths, wagonmakers, boatmen, mechanics, wheelwrights, ect. In the 1920'S Confederate pensions were finally allowed to those workers that were still living. Many thousands more served in other Confederate States.

Confederate blacks' role overlooked

By Dan Sewell | *Associated Press*

Sunday, February 21, 1999

ATLANTA -- Like other members of the Sons of Confederate Veterans, Emerson Emory says he wants to preserve his Southern heritage. His mission, however, is especially challenging -- and controversial.

The 74-year-old Dallas psychiatrist is black, and his insistence that many black Southerners not only supported the Confederacy but also fought for it in the Civil War often draws reactions ranging from skepticism to outrage.

"Most of the reaction was among my friends in the black race -- they couldn't understand," Mr. Emory said. "I think it's one of those things that they don't want to hear anything about."

While recognition of the role black soldiers played for the Union -- dramatized in the movie *Glory* -- has grown in the past decade, there remains little recognition -- or even acknowledgment -- of black Confederates.

Charles Kelly Barrow, a Zebulon, Ga., high school teacher who is white, has spent years researching blacks in the Confederacy. Besides many disbelieving blacks, he said, there are whites who don't want to admit that blacks fought for the South.

"They're in opposition either way. Certain people have always tried to divide white and black Southerners," he said.

Mr. Barrow's 1995 book, *Forgotten Confederates*, is an anthology that draws upon wartime newspaper accounts, later accounts of Civil War reunions, essays, obituaries and pension records to offer evidence of blacks serving the Confederacy.

Some Southern heritage buffs estimate their numbers at anywhere from 38,000 to 90,000 men, mainly serving as laborers, teamsters, musicians and cooks.

As early as 1863, Confederate Maj. Gen. Patrick Cleburne urged that blacks be enlisted as soldiers. There was opposition from Confederates who questioned whether men serving as soldiers could be returned to slavery after the war and who would work the region's farms if slaves were taken away.

In March 1865, the Confederate Congress authorized black soldiers, but there's little indication that any all-black Confederate units went to war.

However, there are accounts that, from the war's beginning, blacks in gray sometimes were armed in battle.

Besides examples of loyalty and even bravery on behalf of the Confederacy, Southern heritage buffs also note that there were no wide slave insurrections during the war.

However, those on the other side of the debate point to the thousands of slaves who fled to the North and joined the fight against the Rebels. Many of those who remained behind likely did so out of fear and an expectation that they would soon be free regardless, they say.

"As the star of the Confederacy waned, the Negroes within its shrinking orbit continued to enact the roles in which they had cast themselves," wrote Morgan State College professor Benjamin Quarles in his 1953 book, *The Negro in the Civil War*. "They were convinced that the fated hour of freedom was drawing nearer by the minute."

A servant to Maj. Raleigh Spinks Camp of the 40th Georgia Infantry of the Amry of Tennessee, indentified only as Marlboro is shown in this Civil War-era photo.

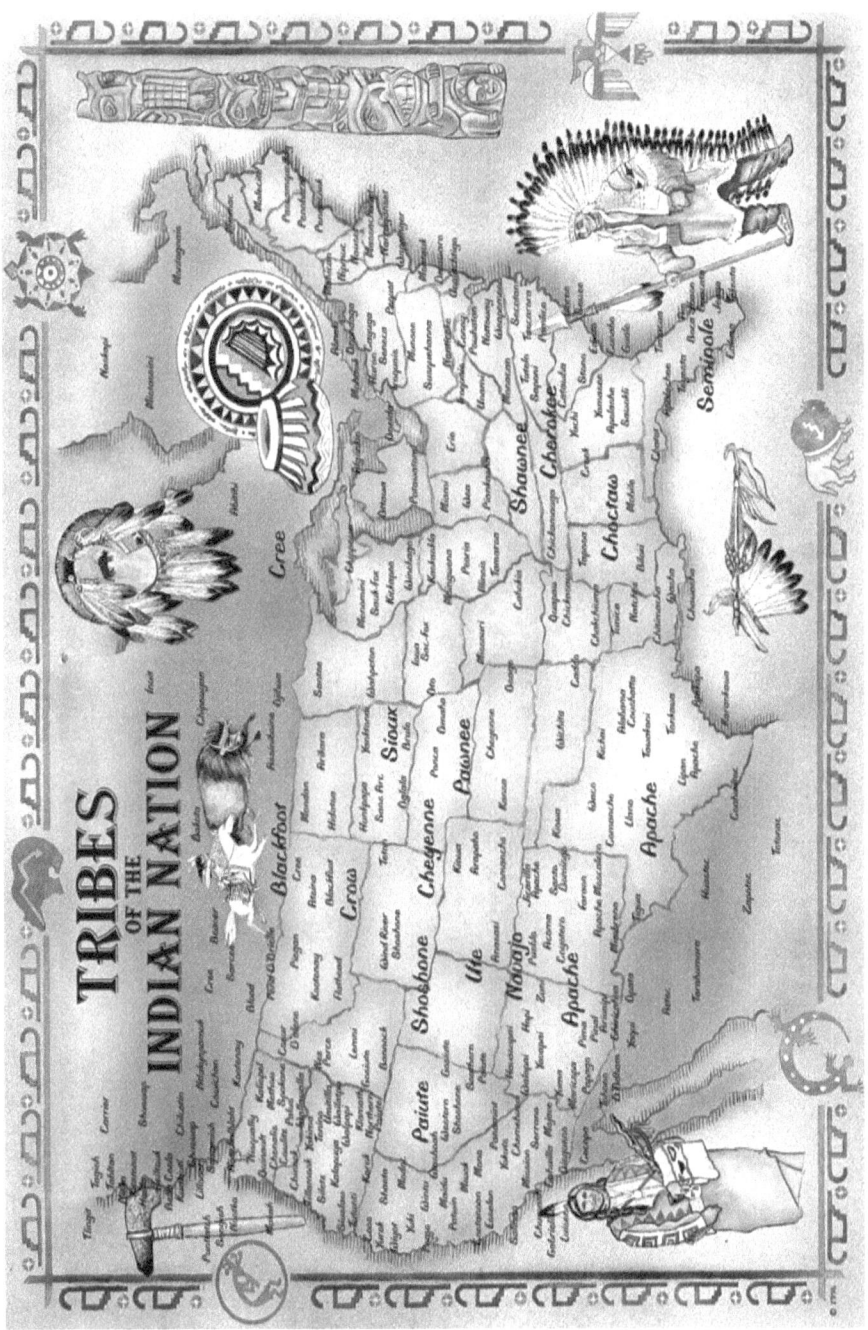

BLACK HISTORY MONTH
BLACK CONFEDERATE HERITAGE

This fact sheet is prepared by the Sons of Confederate Veterans Education Committee for distribution to professors, teachers, librarians, principals, ethnic leaders, members of the press, and others interested in promoting an understanding of Black contributions to United States history. The SCV hopes this information will enrich the celebration of Black History Month during February. This sheet may be freely copied and distributed without permission or notice; if republished in part or whole, please credit the Sons of Confederate Veterans.

"There are at the present moment, many colored men in the Confederate Army doing duty... as real soldiers, having muskets on their shoulders and bullets in their pockets...." Frederick Douglas, former slave & abolitionist (Fall 1861)

How many? Easily tens of thousands of blacks served the Confederacy as laborers, teamsters, cooks and even as soldiers. Some estimates indicate 25% of free blacks and 15% of slaves actively supported the South during the war.

Why? Blacks served the South because it was their home, and because they hoped for the reward of patriotism for these reasons they fought in every war through Korea, even though it meant defending a segregated United States.

Emancipation? President Lincoln's Emancipation Proclamation did not free a single slave. Issued at a time when the Confederacy seemed to be winning the war, Lincoln hoped to transform a disagreement over secession into a crusade against slavery, thus preventing Great Britain (and France) from intervening on the side of the South. The proclamation allowed slavery to continue in the North as well as in Tennessee and large parts of Louisiana and Virginia. It applied only to Confederate-held slaves, which Lincoln had no authority over, but not to slaves under Federal control.

Lincoln's Views? "I am not in favor of making voters or jurors of Negroes, nor of qualifying them to hold office..." 9/15/1858 campaign speech "I have no purpose, directly or indirectly, to interfere with the institution of slavery...." 3/4/1861 First Inaugural Address "I am a little uneasy about the abolishment of slavery in this District [of Columbia]." 3/24/1862 letter to Horace Greeley "If I could save the Union without freeing any slave I would do it...." 8/22/1862 letter to Horace Greeley, New York Tribune editor

Confederate: Famed bridge engineer and former slave Horace King received naval contracts for building Confederate warships. A black servant named Sam Ashe killed the first Union officer during the war, abolitionist Major Theodore Winthrop. John W. Buckner, a black private, was wounded at Ft. Wagner repulsing the U.S. (Colored) 54th Massachusetts Regiment. George Wallace, a servant who surrendered with General Lee at Appomattox later served in the Georgia Senate. Jim Lew's served General Stonewall Jackson, and was honored to hold his horse "Little Sorrel" at

1865-Present

108

THE MOORISH CONFEDERATE REPUBLIC

A.K.A
The Five Great Nations

Cherokees, Choctaws, Chickasaws, Creeks and Seminoles

confederacy of states

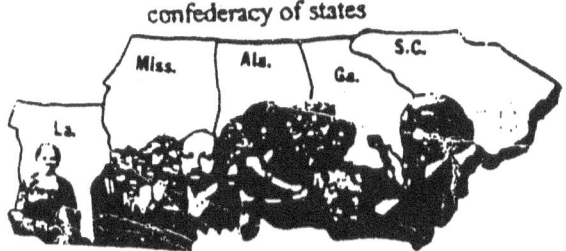

Five Civilized Tribes

The Five Civilized Tribes was a loose confederation, formed in 1859, of North American Indians in what was then INDIAN TERRITORY (in present-day Oklahoma). The group comprised the Iroquoian-speaking CHEROKEE and the Muskogean-speaking CHICKASAW, CHOCTAW, CREEK, and SEMINOLE. They were described as "civilized" because of their early adoption of many of the white man's ways. Under the Indian Removal Act of 1830, the Five Tribes were deported from their traditional homelands east of the Mississippi and forced to settle in Indian Territory. Each organized an autonomous state modeled after the U.S. federal government, established courts and a formalized code of laws, constructed schools and Christian churches, and developed a writing system patterned on the one earlier devised by the Cherokee.

Intro: They were called "civilized tribes" because they embraced American ways. They were the Chickasaws and Choctaws of Mississippi, the Cherokee and Creeks of Alabama and Georgia, the Seminoles of Florida. But their attempts to mirror American society did not alter the U.S. policy of *Removal* that uprooted them from their homes and resulted in the sorrowful Trail of Tears.

THE CREATION PROCESS IN AMERICA

THE CONFEDERACY

States which seceded from the Union on 20 December 1860: Alabama (Montgomery capitol of the CSA until 1863), Florida, Georgia, Louisiana, Mississippi, South Carolina, Texas

on 11 April 1860, following the firing on Fort Sumter: Kentucky, Tennessee, Virginia (Richmond capitol of CSA from 1863 until the end of the war in 1865).

BLACK NATION
confederacy of states

Articles of Confederation

Constitution for the United States of America

↓

The United States of America (USA) and the Confederate States of America (CSA)

Hiram Revels of Mississippi became the first African American senator in 1870. Born in North Carolina in 1827, Revels attended Knox College in Illinois and later served as minister in the African Methodist Episcopal Church in Baltimore, Maryland. He raised two black regiments during the Civil War and fought at the battle of Vicksburg in Mississippi. The Mississippi state legislature sent him to fill a vacancy in the U.S. Senate during Reconstruction, and he quickly became an outspoken opponent of racial segregation. Although Revels' term in the Senate lasted just a year, he broke new ground for African Americans in Congress.

http://www.senate.gov/artandhistory/history/common/generic/Featured_Bio_Revels.htm

AMERICA: Land of The MOORS

John Horse, Leader of the Seminoles for more than thirty years.

Blanche K. Bruce

U.S. Senate, Mississippi

In the Senate, Bruce was a member of the committees on Pensions, Manufactures, and Education and Labor. He chaired the Committee on River Improvements and the Select Committee to Investigate the Freedman's Savings and Trust Company. Bruce encouraged increasing the disposition of western land grants to African Americans. On February 14, 1879, Bruce became the first African American to preside over the Senate.

Born into slavery in 1841, Blanche Kelso Bruce became the first African American to serve a full term in the U.S. Senate, as well as the first African American to preside over the Senate. Just 20 years old when the Civil War began, Bruce tried to enlist in the Union army. At that time, the army did not accept black recruits, so Bruce turned to teaching; he later organized the first school in Missouri for African Americans. In 1869 Bruce moved to Mississippi to become a cotton planter. Active in Mississippi Republican politics, he served as supervisor of elections, tax assessor, sheriff, superintendent of education, and sergeant at arms of the state senate. In 1874 the Mississippi legislature elected him to the U.S. Senate where he served until 1881.

After leaving the Senate, Bruce was appointed registrar of the U.S. Treasury by President James Garfield. At the Republican convention of 1888, Bruce received 11 votes for vice president. He was appointed recorder of deeds for the District of Columbia and later was a member of the board of trustees of Howard University.

http://www.senate.gov/artandhistory/art/artifact/Painting_32_00039.htm

Robert B. Elliott
U.S. Congressman, S. Carolina

One of the South's most brilliant political organizers during Reconstruction, Robert B. Elliott (1842-1884) appears to have been born in Liverpool, England, of West Indian parents and was educated in England, graduating from Eton College in 1859. He came to Boston on an English naval vessel shortly after the Civil War.

After moving to South Carolina in 1867, Elliott established a law practice and helped to organize the Republican party. He "knew the political condition of every nook and corner throughout the state," said one political ally.

Elliott served in the constitutional convention of 1868 and the state legislature, and was twice elected to Congress.

He resigned in 1874 to fight political corruption in South Carolina, where he became Speaker of the House.

In Congress, Elliott delivered a celebrated speech in favor of the bill that became the Civil Rights Act of 1875, which prohibited discrimination in public accommodations because of race. Elliott himself had been denied service in a restaurant while traveling to Washington.

In 1881, Elliott headed a delegation that met with president-elect James A. Garfield to complain that with the end of Reconstruction, Southern blacks were "citizens in name and not in fact."

Because of his role in politics, Elliott's law practice was boycotted by white patrons.

http://www.digitalhistory.uh.edu/exhibits/reconstruction/section4/section4_27.html

The Members of the 41st and 42nd Congress of the United States- Standing are: Representatives Robert C. De Large of South Carolina, and Jefferson H. Long of George. Sitting from left to right: Senator of the United States H. R. Revels of Mississippi, and four other Representatives: Benjamin S. Tuner of Alabama, Josiah T. Walls of Florida, Joseph H. Rainey and R. Brown Elliott, the second Grand Master of the P. H. G. L. of South Carolina.

Moorish CHEROKEES

Noble Drew Ali

Through sin and disobedience every nation has suffered slavery, due to the fact that they honored not the creed and principles of their forefathers. That is why the nationality of the Moors was taken away from them in 1774 and the word negro, black and colored, was given to the Asiatics of America who were of Moorish descent, because they honored not the principles of their mother and father, and strayed after the gods of Europe of whom they knew nothing. [from *The Circle 7 Koran.*]

One Cherokee who moved west in 1829 was one of America's most honored Indians, **Sequoyah**. He was intrigued with the white man's ability to write, so after 12 years of experimenting and study, Sequoyah created an 86-letter syllabary for the Cherokee language. This alphabet was so efficient it could be learned in less than a month and became the standard means of communication for the Cherokee. Sequoyah's home is still standing near Sallisaw.

 1865

The American Civil War ends. During the war, the "scorched earth" policy of the North destroyed churches, farms, schools, libraries, colleges, and a great deal of other property. The libraries at the University of Alabama managed to save one book from the debris of their library buildings. On the morning of April 4, when Federal troops reached the campus with order to destroy the university, Andre Deloffre, a modern language professor and custodian of the library, appealed to the commanding officer to spare one of the finest libraries in the South. The officer, being sympathetic, sent a courier to Gen. Croxton at his headquarters in Tuscaloosa asking permission to save the Rotunda. The general's reply was no. The officer reportedly said, "I will save one volume as a memento of this occasion. The volume selected was a rare copy of the Qur'an.

1866

The last Cherokee Indian chief was Ramadhan Ibn Wati (popularly known as Stand Watie, 1806-71). He was the last Confederate general to surrender his command to the United States on June 23, 1865. His son **Saladin Watie** served on Southern Cherokee delegation to Washington to sign a new treaty with the United States at the end of Civil War. He died mysteriously at the age of 21. (Saladin is an anglicized name for Salahuddin, the famous Sultan who liberated Jerusalem from the crusaders in 1187). Some books published as late as 1832 show Cherokee men wearing turbans and the women wearing long head coverings. A portrait of **Sequoyah**, inventor of Cherokee Alphabets consisting of 86 characters (1821).

Stand Watie

ENTITLED *"UNDER THE VEIL,"* THE ILLUSTRATION IS A CIVIL WAR-ERA ENGRAVING BY AUSTRIAN-BORN ARTIST ADALBERT VOLCK. VOLCK WAS A CONFEDERATE SYMPATHIZER WHO LIVED IN BALTIMORE MARYLAND AND MADE THIS CARICATURE IN SEPTEMBER OF 1862. IT WAS AROUND THE TIME OF LINCOLN'S FAMED "EMANCIPATION PROCLAMATION" WHICH FREED SLAVES IN REBEL STATES. LINCOLN'S OBVIOUS AFRICOID APPEARANCE IN THIS IMAGE WAS INTENDED TO AGAIN ATTACK HIS LINEAGE. MANY OF MR. LINCOLN'S CONTEMPORARIES THOUGHT THE PRESIDENT TO BE OF AFRICAN (OR SO-CALLED *FREE* NEGRO) ANCESTRY VIA HIS BIRTH-MOTHER NANCY HANKS.

BUT WHAT IS MOST UNIQUE ABOUT THIS CARICATURE IS THAT IT DOES NOT DISPLAY THE USUAL GROTESQUE OR BUFFOONISH IMAGERY MOST COMMONLY ASSOCIATED WITH NEGROES/BLACKS. IN FACT, THE IMAGE IS DIGNIFIED AND LARGELY MEANT TO SIMPLY ASSOCIATE LINCOLN WITH AFRICAN LINEAGE. BUT MORE SPECIFICALLY, THE *MOORISH-STYLE* SCIMITAR, PANTALOONS AND SLIPPERS ALL INDICATE THAT VOLCK WAS SPECIFICALLY ASSOCIATING PRESIDENT LINCOLN WITH MOORISH ANCESTRY.

HISTORIAN RUFUS ROCKWELL WILSON TELLS US THAT VOLCK WAS RUN OUT OF BALTIMORE AND HAD TO FLEE TO EUROPE, WHEN THIS AND OTHER PLATES WERE DISCOVERED BY UNION GOVERNMENT AGENTS. HIS PLATES WERE THEN CAPTURED AND DESTROYED BEFORE THEY ENJOYED WIDE DISTRIBUTION. VOLCK WOULD LATER RETURN TO THE U.S. IN 1864, AND PUBLISH A PORTFOLIO OF HIS CARICATURES. BUT FOR SOME REASON, HE DID NOT INCLUDE THIS CARTOON. VOLCK'S CARTOON COMPELS US TO WONDER WHETHER THE EUROPEAN-BORN VOLCK KNEW SOMETHING ABOUT THE MOORISH PRESENCE IN THE AMERICAS.

- FROM WILSON'S LINCOLN IN CARICATURE: 165 POSTER CARTOONS AND DRAWINGS FOR THE PRESS (ELMIRA N.Y., 1945).

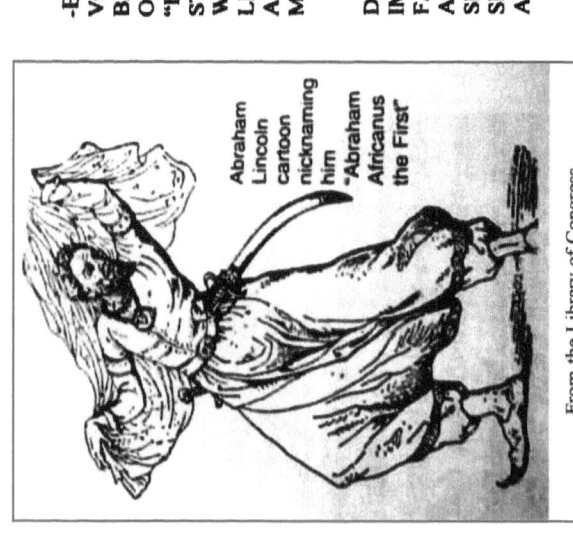

Abraham Lincoln cartoon nicknaming him "Abraham Africanus the First"

From the Library of Congress

WHITE SLAVERY AND THE MOORS
THE HIDDEN HISTORY

I asked the question many years ago to my history teach in my high school era, about something I had noticed about the slavery era. A particular history book caught my attention because it was suggesting that whites such as the Irish people were not only slaves, but were constantly running away from the slave master but also hiding amongst the native people/ Indians.

When I mentioned this fact to my teacher she had not noticed this portion of slave history and when asked to expound on the subject, she mentioned it was called indentured servitude as to say they were not really slaves but the truth is that they were the first to be enslaved and for some time the only slaves.

This is another epic of the blacking out through whitewash. The great American cover up about the truth of slavery in America is that most of the slave stories do not belong to Moors/ black people, but to the Euros, especially Slavs, Poles, and Irish as well as the majority of plantations being owned by black people/ Moors. In the images that follow, you will see some of the hidden truth about Europeans as slaves in America and Africa.

Omari Miles El

White slave in Egypt. (Drawing by Sichel).

mostly women,—the Circassians. One Arab writer declared that Arabia is such a hard country to live in that but for the importation of African and Circassian slaves its population would soon be extinct.

SLAVERY OF WHITES IN AMERICA

It happens, too, that the first slaves in what is now the United States, were white Englishmen. The earliest warrants banishing convicts to a life of servitude in Virginia were signed by James I in 1617 and the first hundred arrived in 1619 (that is, the same year the Negroes did), and were sold.

The Greek Slave by Hiram Powers.

The Campaign for Radical Truth in History http://www.hoffman-info.com

P.O. Box 849, Coeur d'Alene, Idaho 83816

The following article is a brief synopsis of the extensive research found in Michael A. Hoffman II's ground-breaking history book, "They Were White and They Were Slaves."

The Forgotten Slaves: Whites in Servitude in Early America and Industrial Britain

White children enslaved in a mine in 19th century England. The two on the left are virtually naked. Children of both sexes worked in this manner.

by Michael A. Hoffman II ©Copyright 1999. All Rights Reserved

Two years ago, Prime Minister Paul Keating of Australia refused to show "proper respect" to Britain's Queen Elizabeth II during her state visit. In response, Terry Dicks, a Conservative member of the British Parliament said, "It's a country of ex-convicts, so we should not be surprised by the rudeness of their prime minister."

http://www.revisionisthistory.org/forgottenslaves.html

When Hell Was In Session

"Their bodies and souls are used as if hell commenced here and only continued in the world to come." -Sir Thomas Montgomery in a letter to the Lords of Trade and Plantations on the suffering of enslaved White people, August 3, 1688.

Did You Know

+ That the laws governing Black slavery were originally devised to regulate the traffic in White people.

+ That between one-half to two-thirds of all the arrivals in the American colonies were White slaves, many of them children "kid-napped" in Britain.

+ That Whites were auctioned on the block, with children sold and separated from their parents and wives sold and separated from their husbands.

+ That the death-rates for White slaves in the Middle Passage to America were greater than that of Black slaves.

+ That Fugitive Slave Laws were first enacted to apprehend runaway Whites who upon capture were branded, whipped, mutilated, burned alive or hung.

+ That four-fifths of the White slaves sent to the sugar colonies did not survive the first year.

Michael A. Hoffman II's thoroughly researched challenge to the conventional historiography of colonial labor is a stunning journey into a heretofore hidden epoch-- the Atlantic slave trade *in Whites* -- kidnapped, chained, whipped and worked to death in the millions. This is a chronicle that has never been told, part of a vital heritage that has until now comprised the dustiest shelf in the darkest corner of suppressed American history.

I was unhappily Trepan'd;
...Not then a slave....
But things are changed...Kidnap'd and Fool'd..."

The height of academic and media fraud is revealed in the monopolistic trademark status the official controllers of education and mass communications have successfully established between the definition of the word "slave" and the negro, while labeling descriptions of the historic experience of Whites in slavery a fallacy. Yet the very word "slave" which the establishment's consensus school of history pretends cannot legitimately be applied to Whites, comes from the word Slav. According to the Oxford English Dictionary, the word slave is another name for the the White people of eastern Europe, the Slavs. (*Compact Edition of the Oxford English Dictionary*, p. 2,858).

In other words, the word slave itself has always been a term for and a definition of White slaves, not Blacks. Yet we are told by modern historians that it is not proper to refer to Whites as slaves but only as servants, even though the very root of the word is derived from the historical fact of White slavery. (1)

A Holocaust Against The White Poor

White slaves were obtained from the poorest levels of British society. These White human beings existed in conditions of great hardship. The ruling class regarded them as completely expendable.

The English slums of the 17th, 18th and 19th centuries were pits of White suffering. London's St. Giles was known locally as "Rat's Castle." A policeman who worked the area used metaphors from the insect world to describe the conditions of the Whites there, referring to them as "vermin haunted heaps of rags." Opening the door to a tiny shack the policeman discovered:

"Ten, twenty, thirty--who can count them? Men, women, children, for the most part naked, heaped upon the floor like maggots in a cheese...a spectral rising, unshrouded, from a grave of rags." ("On Duty with Inspector Field," In *Household Words*, June 14, 1851, pp. 265-267).

Herman Melville, in his autobiographical account of his first voyage as a sailor, described the same living death in the English port city of Liverpool in 1839:

"...I generally passed through a narrow street called 'Launcelott's-Hey...once passing through this place...I heard a feeble wail...it seemed the low, hopeless, endless wail of someone forever lost."

"At last I advanced to an opening...to deep tiers of cellars beneath a crumbling old warehouse; and there, some fifteen feet below the walk, crouching in nameless squalor, with her head bowed over, was the figure of what had been a woman.

"Her blue arms folded to her livid bosom two shrunken things like children that leaned toward her, one on each side. At first, I knew not whether they were alive or dead...They were dumb and next to dead with want. How they had crawled into that den, I could not tell; but there they had crawled to die.

"...I tried to lift the woman's head; but feeble as she was, she seemed bent upon holding it down. Observing her arms clasped upon her bosom, and that something seemed hidden under the rags there, a thought crossed my mind which impelled me forcibly to withdraw her hands for a moment when I caught glimpse of a meager little babe, the lower part of its body thrust into an old bonnet.

"Its face was dazzling white, even in its squalor; but the closed eyes looked like balls of indigo. It must have been dead some hours...I stood looking down on them, while my whole soul swelled within me; and I asked myself, what right had any body in the wide world to smile and be glad when sights like this were to be seen?" (Melville, *Redburn: His First Voyage*, Anchor Books edition, pp. 173-178).

Charles Darwin's uncle, factory owner Josiah Wedgewood, owned a business that worked White children of five years of age in a chemical factory permeated with lead oxide, a deadly poison. Wedgewood acknowledged that the lead made the children "very subject to disease" but worked them anyway.

The English writer Frances Trollope estimated that at least 200,000 English children were "snatched away" to factories, "...taken and lodged amid stench, and stunning, terrifying tumult; driven to and fro until their little limbs bend under them...the repose of a moment to be purchased only by yielding their tender bodies to the fist, the heel or the strap of the overlooker (overseer)." (Marcus Cunliffe, *Chattel Slavery and Wage Slavery*, p. 73).

In 1723 the Waltham Act was passed which classified more than 200 minor offenses such as stealing a rabbit from an aristocrat or breaking up his fishpond, a crime punishable by

119

MVLEY ARSHEID ZERIFF PRINCE OF
TAFFELETA
EMPEROUR OF MAROCCO AND FEZZ etc.

Moulay al-Rashid (1631-1672) Sultan of Morocco 1666-1672, founder of the Alaouite Dynasty.

Emperor of Morocco, whose mother was an unmixed Negro slave had tens of thousands of white slaves. From a painting of 1670. See John Ogilby's Africa (p. 264, 1670).

Africans treated their white slaves much better than white Americans their Africans. "The meanest Christian slave on becoming a Mohammedan," says Blake, "was free . . . and he and his descendants were eligible to the highest offices in the state." Acceptance of Christianity made no difference in the status of the African slave in America. General Eaton, American consul at Tunis, said in 1799, "Truth and justice demand from me the confession that the Christian slaves among the barbarians of Africa are treated with more humanity than the African slaves among the Christians of civilized America." (Quoted by W. O. Blake, "History of Slavery In Northern Africa," p. 79. 1857).

For centuries also and well into the last century, the Arabs, a Negroid people, had been raiding what is now Russia for white slaves,

European girl captured by Moorish sea-captain. From Voltaire's Candide. Daughter of the Princess of Palestrina. (Illustration by Bruneschelli).

Cave Canem (Beware of Dog) Jene-Leon Gerome

Black Egyptian queen, Nefertari, "one of the most venerated figures" of Egyptian history, is pictured

One item that can be seen here in this reprint of Egyptian fresco is that in the middle row, Cretans Keftiu, like the Egyptians, bring gifts to Pharaoh, that best in a people that is, but the difference is that their gifts are made with very high technical and artistic value than those of other peoples. This shows the high culture that Minoans ancestors had compared to the rest of the known world. This mapping clearly shows us the difference with the peoples of the region.

ISLAM BEFORE COLUMBUS AND DURING THE ANTEBELLUM AMERICA

THE PLAN WAS TO HIDE OR DISTORT THE FACTS THAT AMERICA BRFORE THE SO CALLED FOUNDING FATHERS AND EVEN BEFORE COLUMBUS WAS A MUSLIM COUNTRY GOVERNED UNDER THE ORDER OF ISLAM AND THE HOLY KORAN.

WE ARE TOLD THAT AMERICA IS A CHRISTIAN COUNTRY AND THAT IT WAS FOUNDED ON BIBLICAL PRICIPALS AND, CONGRESS EVEN DECLARED THE BIBLE THE LAW OF THE LAND IN THE FOURTIES.

THE ONLY PRICIPALS PRACTICE FROM THE BIBLE I F ANY WAS WHERE THE SO CALLED JEWS DESTROYED THE CANNANITES AND TOOK THERE LAND UNDER THE DECLARATION OF THERE GOD. HINT

THE FACTS ARE THAT ISLAM FLORISHED THROUGH OUT THE AMERICA'S AND THE AJOINING ISLANDS IT BUT THE HIS-STORIANS OF THE DAY WOULD HAVE YOU BELIEVE THAT ISLAM CAME INTO THE AMERICA'S BY WAY OF THE SLAVE TRADE, WHICH IS WHY THEY RAP ISLAM AROUND THE ANTEBELLUM PERIOD.

WITH THE COMING OF THE INFORMATION AGE THE EVIDENCE IS NOW EASLY ACCESSABLE,THERE ARE MANY SCHOLARS SUCH AS IVAN VAN SERTIMA, BARRY FELL, ALEXANDER VON WUTHENAU, YOUSSEF MROUCH AND MANY OTHERS WHO HAVE SHOWN THESE FACTS IN GREAT DETAIL, AS WELL AS MANY DOCUMENTS LOCATED IN THE CONGRESSIONAL RECORDS, LIBRARY OR CONGRESS, AND THE ARCHIVES, SUCH AS THE U.S. TREATY WITH TRIPOLY WICH SAYS THAT AMERICA WAS FOUNDED ON ISLAM.

Omari Miles El

There is another work which is part of the Old Testament, designated as "JE" which is combination of the "J" priesthood and the "E" priesthood.

It became obvious that this work was done by someone from Judah who had both the works of came into contact or possession of the works of "E" coming from "Israel" with the remnants of Israel who came to Judah after Israel was destroyed by the Assyrian king Sennacherib in 722 BCE.

"P" = PRIESTLY CODE, ALTERNATIVE TO COMBINED JE

It was found that there was another work which focused on the priesthood and was designated "P", which stands for the "priestly code" since this work dealt primarily with issues involving and promoting the priesthood.

R = REDACTOR = EZRA

Last but not least, you have the person who came into the possession of all of these works, as well as, Babylonian and Persian histories and religion, while in exile in Babylon, and redacted, compiled, edited and published what has become known as the "Torah" or "Old Testament". This person is designated as "R" or the redactor, and is none other than Ezra. We will have more in the next issue.

Ancient Place Names in the United States That Exist To This Day

See if you can find; Morocco, Tunis, Algiers, Moab, Mecca, Arabia, Turkey, Tripoli, Atlantis, Patmos, Egypt, Turkey, Sudan, Dahomey, Zion, etc. Coincidence? I'll let you be the judge.

ANCIENT NAME	NAME AFTER 1865
Sea of Galilee	Lake Erie
Bethlehem	Pittsburgh
England	New Jersey, Virginia, & Delaware
Murgill Morocco	Virginia
Spain	New Mexico, Arkansas, Arizona, Wyoming, & Utah
Ali Bumar	Alabama
Moabite	Mobile
House of Canaan	Baltimore, Maryland
Russian	South Dakota
France	Missouri
Paris	St. Louis
China	North Dakota
Moslem Prison	Island of Albine
Egypt	Ohio River to the South
France	East Coast
Was known as S.E. Asia by the Moors	Modern Africa
Mt. Calvary	Capitol Hill
Magna Charter Hall	Constitutional Hall
The Knowledge is in Reserve	Western Reserve

MODERN NAME	ANCIENT NAME
Novia Scotia	Ancient Scotland
New York State	Germany
Virginia	England
California	Spain and Japan
Montana	Spain
Alabama	Egypt
Louisiana	Algeria
Ohio (Cleveland)	Libya
Sandusky	Antioch
Chicago	Mecca
Detroit	Medina
Venezuela	Rome
Argentina	Europe (Original)

Niagra Falls—Implies 50,000 Moorish women who were beheaded. Several wars in the Bible and in history occurred in North America.

Bible Verification:

>Says Jesus to the Roman priesthood:
>Think not I am come to destroy the law
>or the prophets. I am not come to destroy
>but to fulfill. For verily I say unto you, till
>heaven and earth pass one jot or one title
>shall in no wise pass from the law till all be fulfilled.
>*Matthew 5:17, 18*

This prophesy or scripture means that every tongue must confess and every knee must bow to the 12 zodiac signs foundation of God's Divine Law of the Universe. Here you are referred to Revelation, the 21st Chapter, Verses 2–5, and 10—14 to research Bible verification of zodiac universe prophesy. in operation to fulfill with the U.S.A. In this day and time to restore the so-called Negro its inherited Moorish Nationality, Birthright, and Divine Law of the 12 Zodiac Signs foundation with three signs of the West Gate, three of the North, three of the East Gate, three of the South Gate. *Revelations 21:13 and 14.*

There is another work which is part of the Old Testament, designated as "JE" which is combination of the "J" priesthood and the "E" priesthood.

It became obvious that this work was done by someone from Judah who had both the works of came into contact or possession of the works of "E" coming from "Israel" with the remnants of Israel who came to Judah after Israel was destroyed by the Assyrian king Sennacherib in 722 BCE.

"P" = PRIESTLY CODE, ALTERNATIVE TO COMBINED JE

It was found that there was another work which focused on the priesthood and was designated "P", which stands for the "priestly code" since this work dealt primarily with issues involving and promoting the priesthood.

R = REDACTOR = EZRA

Last but not least, you have the person who came into the possession of all of these works, as well as, Babylonian and Persian histories and religion while in exile in Babylon, and redacted, compiled, edited and published what has become known as the "Torah" or "Old Testament". This person is designated as "R" or the redactor, and is none other than Ezra. We will have more in the next issue.

Ancient Place Names in the United States That Exist To This Day

See if you can find; Morocco, Tunis, Algiers, Moab, Mecca, Arabia, Turkey, Tripoli, Atlantis, Patmos, Egypt, Turkey, Sudan, Dahomey, Zion, etc. Coincidence? I'll let you be the judge.

c/o Mu-Atlantis P.O. Box 980, Baychester St., Bx. NY 1046-0705 / www.mu-atlantis.com / ©1996-2001

MODERN NAMES	ANCIENT NAMES
Nova Scotia	Ancient Scotland
New York State	Germany
Virginia	England
California	Spain & Japan
Montana	Spain
Alabama	Egypt
Louisiana	Algeria
Ohio	Libya
Sandusky	Antioch
Chicago	Mecca
Detroit	Medina
Venezuela	Rome
Argentina	Europe (Original)

Niagara Falls – 50,000 Moorish women had their heads cut off. All wars in the Bible and history occurred in North America.

CUSH...Son of Ham (Gen.x.6); Ethiopia (Ez. xxxix. 10; 2 Chr. xii. 3). (Jer. xxiii. 23)

"**CUSCATLAN**", biblio. ref., see: Netscape website:
"*500 Years Of Indigenous Resistance*", p.1 – Pre-Columbian America

NAMES IN AMERICA OF MOORISH / MOSLEM DECENT

AMERICA------------- AMIR AMER EMEER ICA-IKUS

CALIFORNIA---------KHALIFAH

CAROLINA------------CAR-KAR-KOR-KORAN-KORSHITES= CHILDREN OF THE GODDESS CAR

ALABAMA------------ALI-BA –MU

MOBILE----------------MU-BA-EL

SHERIFF----------------SHARIFF

TALLAHSEE----------TA-ALLAH-SEE

MUSLIM LEGACY IN EARLY AMERICAS
West Africans, Moors and Amerindians

Jose V. Pimienta-Bey

- Introduction
- Barry Fell
- Alexander Von Wuthenau
- Ivan Van Sertima
- De Lacy O'Leary
- Caribbean, Panama and Columbia
- Clyde Ahmad Winters
- Moorish Heritage

Introduction

The works of men such as Ivan Van Sertima, Barry Fell and Alexander Von Wuthenau represent 20th century scholarship which has stated directly or indirectly - that there has been a significant Muslim presence in the early Americas. While it is true that there have been a number of Muslim writers such as Clyde-Ahmad Winters who have sought to enlighten folks to that fact, it is perhaps more significant that "non-Muslims" have conceded such evidence of pre and post-Colombian Muslims on this continent.

Barry Fell

New Zealand archaeologist and linguist Barry Fell [Howard Barraclough ("Barry") Fell] in his work *Saga America (1980)* pointed to existing evidence of a Muslim presence in various parts of the Americas. In addition to drawing several cultural parallels between West African peoples and certain "Indian" peoples of the southwest, Fell points out that the southwest's Pima people possessed a vocabulary which contained words of Arabic origin. The presence of such words among the Pima is compounded by the existence of Islamic petroglyphs in places like California. Fell informs us that in Inyo county, California, there exists an early American petrogyph (rock carving) which stated in Arabic: "Yasus ben Maria" ("Jesus, Son of Mary"), a phrase commonly found within the **surahs of the Holy Qur'an**. Fell is convinced that this glyph is many centuries older than the U.S.

Fell also identified the *algonquian language* as having words with arabic roots, especially words

which pertained to navigation, astronomy, meteorology, medicine and anatomy. The presence of such words again illustrates significant cultural contact between the American "Indians" and the Arabic-speaking peoples of the Islamic world. Such Islamic peoples evidently came primarily from the African continent as additional evidence suggests.

Alexander Von Wuthenau

Although German art historian and collector Alexander Von Wuthenau argues that the ancient and early Americas were filled with an international melange of peoples from Africa, Asia and Europe, his artifactual evidence reveals that Islamic peoples were clearly a prominent group within it. In his classic work, *Unexpected Faces in Ancient America (1975)*, Von Wuthenau specifically identifies a group of carved heads as "Moorish-looking." Found within Mexico, such heads are dated between 300 - 900 C.E. and another between 900 -1500 C.E. (common era). One such artifact of the "classic" (300 - 900 C.E.) is described by Von Wuthenau as "an old man with hat." Such artifacts are worth a thousand words and the photograph of the "old man" artifact clearly resembles that of an old man wearing a Fez.

The presence of the naja among the dineh (a.k.a. "Navjo") is intriguing given the other evidence of Islamic contacts with the early American west. The naja is a crescent moon symbol found among the dineh that is used in such things as decoration and jewelry. While it is indeed possible that the symbol was indigenous to the dineh, a number of Smithsonian scholars apparently think that the symbol: "spread from Moslem North Africa to Spain, then to Mexico, then to the Navajo" (*The Native Americans (1991)* edited by **Colin Taylor**). Although the inference of the Smithsonian published text seems to be that the Spaniards brought the naja, it seems very odd to me that the crucifix-centered Catholic Spaniards would introduce such a symbol. After all, the customarily dogmatic Catholic Spaniards would have been introducing a religious symbol which represented the spiritual motif of their nemesis. If it was brought from Spain, I would argue that it probably came via expelled Moorish Muslims or subjugated "Moriscos." "Morisco" was the term used by Catholic officials to designate Moors (Moros) who were allowed to re main in Catholic dominions. It is essentially pejorative.

Ivan Van Sertima

Ivan Van Sertima is of course renowned for his first revitalizing original work: *They Came Before Columbus (1976)* which outlined evidence of ancient and early African contacts with the American continent. Although it was not the first work to discuss the topic, it certainly consolidated the African evidence in a more interdisciplinary fashion which cried out for renewed attention particularly from the African American community. Van Sertima's other edited works like *African Presence In Early America* offered additional information about the African legacy in the Americas. Both of the above works point out proofs of African Muslim settlements/contacts within the *pre-Columbian* Americas. Van Sertima identifies 12th and 13th century Chinese documents which spoke of "Arab" Muslim trade extending beyond the Atlantic coast of west Africa

Among the items of evidence which Van Sertima unveils is the presence of African Muslim surnames among American "Indian" peoples. Quoting a French linguist, Van Sertima points out that *Ges, Zamoras, Marabitine,* and *Marabios* are a few of the names with clear transcontinental links. Of particular interest to me, however, are the names "Marabitine" and "Marabios" which I noted relate to "Marabout" (Murabit): the "Holy Men and Women" of the Moorish Empire. The **Marabouts** were the protectors of African Muslim frontiers, they are often remembered for having acted as buffers against Catholic/European encroachment. The famed **Ibn Battuta** spoke of the Marabouts in his renowned "*Travels*." The antiquity of such a "Moorish" (African) presence in the Americas is hereby seen to be quite early when one considers the significance of all the evidence presented here-to-for.

De Lacy O'Leary

In his work *Arabic Thought and It's Place In Western History (1992)*, the late British "Orientalist" De Lacy O'Leary also spoke of the area of "western Maghreb" extending "beyond the Atlantic" during the pre-Columbian Islamic era. The question is how far did O'Leary mean? Although O'Leary never clearly states that there was an Islamic presence in the early Americas, his inference compels us to wonder if that is what he meant but was not willing to say overtly. As a scholar of the Islamic world, De Lacy certainly knew that Muslims possessed the organizational, technical and navigational skill to make such a journey. The historic proof of one such journey comes in the form of **Abu Bakari II** of Mali, who is reported in *Roudh el-kartos* to have made such a trip in the early 14th century (circa 1312 C.E.). This is noted in Van Sertima's *They Came Before Columbus*.

Caribbean, Panama and Columbia

In Panama and Colombia there were rulers ("princes") whom the invading Catholic Spaniards recognized as having "completely Moorish or biblical" names: such as "Do-Bayda" and "Aben-Amechy." This was revealed by the mid-19th century French scholar **Brasseur de Bourboug** and is noted in Van Sertima's edited work *African Presence In Early America*.

Even in the Caribbean the evidence of a significant Muslim presence can be found. **P.V. Ramos** points out in his essay in *African Presence in Early America*, that Christopher Columbus' own impression of the "Carib" peoples was that they were "Mohemmedans." Ramos says that the dietary restrictions of the Carib were similar to those of Islamic peoples and this provided one reason for such an impression.

In the post-Columbian era there were large numbers of Muslims residing within the European colonized Americas. Brother Clyde Ahmad Winters in a 1978 issue of *Al-ittihad: A Quarterly Journal of Islamic Studies*, points outs that large numbers of enslaved Muslims were brought to "Latin America" by (and for) the conquering Catholic authorities of Spain and Portugal. Among the African Islamic peoples which Winters identifies as having been brought to "Latin" territories were the Manding, Fula, Wolof, Berbers and Moors.

The African Muslims of early Latin America were evidently quite successful in converting American Indians to the religion of Islam. Initially allowed to publicly practice their faith, by 1543 Muslims in Spanish controlled American colonies were being expelled from them. Winters informs us that just after an anti-Spanish (Catholic) rebellion of combined Carib and Wolof forces failed in 1532, the Wolof were prohibited from entering the "Latin" Caribbean without special permission from Spanish Catholic authorities. According to Winters, the spread of the Islamic religion among American Indians remained a problem for Spain.

Winters draws several cultural connections between Indian peoples such as the Nanticoke and African Muslims like the Mossi. He also discusses the presence of Islam in places like Brazil whose Muslims were most often literate in the Maghrib style of Arabic. His essay clearly reveals the broad presence of Muslims - especially African Muslims - throughout the Americas: north, central and south. Although Brother Winters doesn't speak directly to the question of whether Muslims reached the Americas before the Catholics of Spain and Portugal, I would venture to say that they did. The earlier evidence cited supports the contention that the arrival of Muslim settlers predated that of the Columbus-era Catholics. In fact, I would contend that the use of Moorish Muslim navigators and navigational information had much to do with enabling the Spanish and Portuguese to even reach and settle the Americas.

Moorish Heritage

I consider it most significant that the African peoples which Winters mentions (such as the Manding, Fula, Moors, Wolof and Berbers) all came from within Moorish Imperial boundaries. Historical records reveal that in Africa the Moorish empire once extended as far south as the Senegal river and as far east as the Egyptian border. Historians of the Maghrib like **S.S. Imamuddin** remind us of the vast expanse of territory which was recognized as "Moorish" by centralized governments of earlier centuries. Recognition of that fact included the Western/European world. Consequently, it would have been reasonable in previous centuries for people to consider Manding, Fula also a Moorish, in that such designated peoples came from within Moorish territory. This would all change of course, as the recognized territories of the Moors would shrink over time.

It must be said that those persons known as Latino and/or Spanish more than likely possess the blood of Moorish (African) forebearers. There is most certainly a link between them and the former Muslim rulers of Al-Andalus - later known as the kingdoms of Spain and Portugal. [**The Moors**]. That fact certainly makes it quite difficult for such peoples to be racist against Africans or Muslims. Such Catholic communities should only argue theological differences and never "racial" ones. A Catholic Spaniard or Latino is essentially attempting to skate on melted ice when they try to make an argument of racial supremacy or distinction. In addition, they would be denying the historic fact of the Islamic Moors primary role as scholarly tutors and beacons of civilized society for medieval Spain and Europe.

There is much more which can be said about the legacy of Muslims in the early Americas. But this short essay was only intended to illuminate an area of the Muslim experience which is all too often overlooked. In spite of what the proverbial mainstream Christian community may think, the presence of Muslims in the Americas is much older and much more profound than many of them know (or care to admit).

It is my hope that this essay has served to enlighten and strengthen the faith of all those who earnestly seek truth, and choose to submit to the will of the One and Only Creator - God, **Allah** (SWT). May the spiritual tenets of Love, Truth, Peace, Freedom and Justice guide us all. Peace.

Allah: Allah is the Arabic word for The One and Only God, The Creator and Sustainer of the universe. It is used by the Arab Christians and Jews for the God (Eloh-im in Hebrew; Allaha in Aramaic, the mother tongue of Jesus, pbuh). The word **Allah** does not have a plural or gender. Allah does not have any associate or partner, and He does not beget nor was He begotten. SWT is an abreviation of Arabic words that mean 'Glory Be To Him.'

Copyright © 1996 *The Message*, an ICNA Publication.
Copyright © 1997 The original article was edited and additional notes were inserted by Dr. A. Zahoor.
This article may be reprinted provided no changes are made and all acknowledgments are included.

4

Abd ar-Rahman and His Two Amazing American Journeys

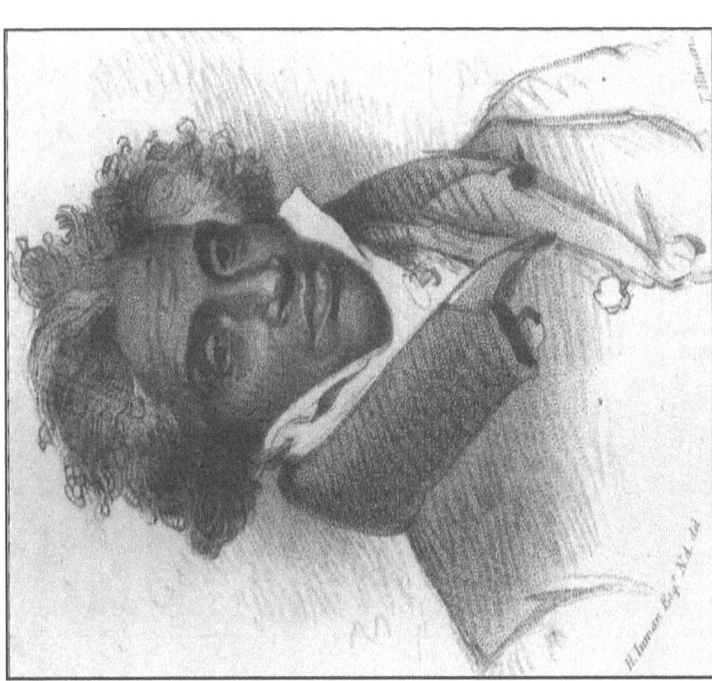

Fig. 10. Ibrahim Abd ar-Rahman, Engraving of Crayon Drawing by Henry Inman, New York, 1828, from *The Colonizationist and Journal of Freedom*, Boston, 1834, frontispiece, photo courtesy of Amherst College.

The year 1828 must have been an exciting one for both the dignified slave "Prince," of Natchez, Mississippi, and the haughty warrior Ibrahim Abd ar-Rahman Jallo, formerly of Timbo, Fura Jallon, Guinea—for they were one and the same man. After forty years of slavery on the American frontier, the six-foot-tall, newly freed sixty-five-year-old was permitted to quit his exile and to begin to make a long way home with his American-born wife, Isabella. As we shall see, this journey was almost a triumphant march in regal costume with himself at the head. Few cities and few dignitaries missed seeing or hearing about the couple or the man. This amazing trip, conducted on steamboats and stagecoaches by way of Cincinnati to Washington, D.C., through three New England states, New York City, Philadelphia, Baltimore, and eventually by boat to Norfolk, Virginia, and then to Liberia, about three hundred miles from his African hometown and nearly six thousand miles from Natchez, took eleven months (April 8, 1828 to March 18, 1829).

How much shorter this voyage must have seemed to the old but dignified, brave man than his trip in the other direction at age twenty-six. At that earlier time, usually in chains, Abd ar-Rahman had been led to the Gambia River and put into the tight and filthy hold of a small slave ship, the *Africa*, which brought him to Dominica Island in the West Indies, from where he was transshipped to New Orleans and then sent by riverboat to Natchez — about six

135

9

Mohammed Ali ben Said, or Nicholas Said: His Travels on Five Continents

This chapter tells about an uncommonly bright, congenial, curious, and adaptable man whose people, the Kanuri; original name, Mohammed Ali ben Said; and references to Allah indicate his African Muslim beginnings. He did not forget the land and the religion of his fathers, as his autobiography shows, but by the time Said arrived in the New World in 1860, he had wandered so far and witnessed so much as both a slave and a freeman that his origins and religion were the oldest parts of his extraordinarily extensive multicultural baggage. The story of Mohammed Ali ben Said, or Nicholas Said, as he called himself after a problematic baptism in Russia, is by any standard an unusual one.

Said was born just west of Lake Chad (present-day Nigeria) into a prosperous military-merchant family around 1833. He was well educated but not wholly wise when he was captured by Tuareg raiders around 1849. Then his travels began. Said was marched as a slave across the Sahara Desert (a three-month trek), was sold in Tripoli and taken to Mecca, became a rich man's slave in Turkey, and was another rich man's manservant in Russia and throughout Europe (1853–1859) before he was hired to be a manservant for a traveler to South and North America. Sometime in 1862, he became a teacher in Detroit, Michigan. A year later, Said joined the 55th Regiment of Massachusetts Colored Volunteers—as deserving of a movie as the more famous 54th, the subject of the film *Glory*. He was mustered out in South Carolina in the fall of 1865. Said married and then disappeared except for a barely legible handwritten note

Fig. 38. **Mohammed Ali or Nicholas Said,** *Carte de Visite*, 1863? *Massachusetts Historical Society, Boston.*

Job Ben Solomon
Born near the Senegal river in Africa, Job's family name suggests direct lineage to King Solomon. Photo from Gentlemen's Magazine (1950), p. 252. Photo from Amherst College.

MOHAMMED ALI BEN SAID: INTERNATIONAL TRAVELER, TEACHER AND LINGUIST

Then there was Mohammed Ali Ben Said. He was a man with an unusual life story. Born around 1831, he was taken from the heart of Africa around 1850, at about 19 years of age. He went from the Mediterranean, to Mecca, and back; served three masters through Europe and part of Asia; and then, as a traveler's companion, made his way to the Caribbean and North and South America.

He had been a traveler on five continents and spoke seven languages. Part of his autobiography has been preserved, and is quoted in the book *African Muslims In Antebellum America*:

I was born in the kingdom of Bornoo, in Soodan, in the problematic central part of Africa, so imperfectly known to the civilized nations of Europe and America. Soodan has several kingdoms, the country of the Fellatahs and Bornoo, being the most powerful, -- the territorial extent of the latter being some 810,000 square miles ... Bornoo has had a romantic history for the last one hundred years. The whole of Soodan, more than two thousand miles in extent, was once under the Mai's of Bornoo; but by dissensions and civil wars nearly all the tributaries north of Lake Tchad were lost. (p. 662, 663)

Mohammed Ali Ben Said was described as "of medium height, somewhat slenderly built, complexion perfectly black, with a quiet, unassuming address." His autobiography was first published in 1867 in the *Atlantic Monthly*, where it appeared under the title "A Native of Bornoo."

Mohammad Ali Ben Said
Born in Bornu in the Sudan, Mohammad Ali Ben Said, renamed "Nicholas" in America, was captured at age 19 during a series of civil wars in his country. He traveled extensively and by 1863 became a teacher in Detroit, Michigan. He first published his autobiography in 1867, after the American Civil War. (Reprinted from African Muslims in Antebellum America, by Allan D. Austin, Copyright 1984, Garland Publishing Company, Inc.)

Also in a Nevada bedrock, Bism Allah "In the name of God" was discovered engraved and decorated with hieroglyphics. Another inscription in large Arabic Kufic letters was uncovered in Nevada by Professor Julian Steward. It read: "Newcomers from Libya".

More evidence: A hoard of Islamic coins have been found in 1787 during road excavations near Cambridge, Massachusetts. These coins were in circulation around the 9th and 11th centuries A.D. and were believed to have been brought to America by Norsemen. The study of the coins is useful because they are easily traced to a particular era or ruler.

Thomas Jefferson's interest in North African Languages

President Thomas Jefferson, as mentioned in Dr. Fell's book, Saga America, was known to encourage the collection of vocabularies by the American consuls stationed in North African countries, particularly in Algeria and Tripoli. He was planning, after his retirement, to publish a book on the linguistic relationships that existed between North Africans and North Americans. His Indian collection of manuscripts and his personal notes on Indian dialects and Berber language were placed in a trunk and shipped from the White House to Monticello. The ship was broken into while it was in route to Monticello. The trunk was stolen by a thief who, after finding no valuables in it, threw it into the James River. Very few manuscripts were saved and sent to Jefferson. His hope to publish the book perished forever.

Now, let's ask ourselves: Did we, as Americans of Arab descent, follow our ancestors' footsteps? The answer is: Yes, of course. This matter is of great interest to us as well as you.

And, let me close this article quoting the words of Dr. Barry Fell of Harvard as written at the end of his book *Saga America*:

"I look to the day when Arab colleagues will climb the Sierra to visit the Hanging Valleys where the name of the prophet lies cut in American bedrock by sailors who found peace there so long ago."

1668
- An Iraqi Chaldean priest ventured to the shores of America for religious reasons.

1790
- The House of Representatives in South Carolina provided that "sundry Moors, Subjects of the Emperor of Morocco," be tried in accord according to the laws for South Carolina citizens and not under Negro codes.

1849
- Omani ship "Sahanah" arrived in New York harbor. Its captain was Ahmad Bin Naaman.

1849
- Father Flavianus Kfoury, a Melkite Catholic priest, of Shweyr, Lebanon, came to the US to collect donations to help rebuild St. John's Convent in Khonchara, Lebanon.

1854
- Antom J. Bishalany officially became the first to enter the United States from an Arab country. He was born in Lebanon in the Metn region in 1827. He was a tourist guide in the Holy Land of Palestine. He died in Brooklyn, NY, 1856, and was buried in the Greenwood Cemetery.

1856
- *Hadji Ali* entered America as a chief cameleer with a shipment of 32 camels ordered by Jefferson Davis, Secretary of War and assigned to the U.S. Army Southern Units. He came to be known as "Hi Jolly". He died in Quartsite, Arizona, 1903. The state of Arizona built a memorial for him (see above).

1869
- The opening of the Suez Canal played a large part in the emigration of Arabs from Yemen to the US. Most came through the port of New York and then made their way west to cities such as Buffalo and Detroit. It is well known that a number of Yemeni sailors jumped ship in San Francisco and settled on the West Coast.

The First Wave 1875-1918

Pay for garment workers was abysmally low, hovering around $10 a week, and women usually received half that. Peddlers often did better, earning between $1,500 and $2,000 a year. They began coming in small groups in the garb of mendicants. They wore red fezzes,

---

1787 - *In the name of God, the merciful. There exists strength and power only by God. From the Servant of God, Mohammed Ibn 'Abd Allah – may God help him – to the President of the United States of America. Salvation be upon him who follows the Righteous Path. We received your letter in which you propose a peace treaty. (We are informing you that) our intention is also to maintain peaceful relations with you. We have also connected Tunis and Tripoli regarding what you solicited from Our Majesty and all your requests will materialize. God willing. Written on the 15th Dhu al-Qa'da 1202 (July 18, 1787)*

7
Umar ibn Said's Legend(s), Life, and Letters

The dignified Abd ar-Rahman and his dramatic story were famous for a year and have been recalled often since. The also dignified, less dramatic, proudly mysterious, even controversial Umar ibn Said and his varied writings were also the objects of attention, from 1819 to 1864—nearly all of Umar's American lifetime—and also into our own time. His Bible in Arabic, a daguerreotype portrait, and fourteen manuscripts in Arabic by Umar have been preserved. These include the only extant autobiography by an American slave in Arabic—a very legible, sixteen-page manuscript. (Abu Bakr as-Siddiq wrote another such autobiography but in Jamaica.) Umar's "Life" was thought to be lost after 1925 but was found late in 1995. Umar's grave has also been rediscovered. There is some debate over the religion of his life and his spirit. Once acclaimed as a convert to Christianity, as an Arabian who found no fault with American slavery and who despised Africans, Umar has recently been more closely examined as a closet Muslim, religiously conservative as his people, the Fulbe clearly African—regularly were. Today, a Quranic school, or *masjid*, in Fayetteville, North Carolina, has been named after Al Hajj Umar ibn Said. In the past, interest in Umar was mostly regional, restricted to the Carolinas, where he lived. About thirty-five articles, including mixes of fact and fiction, surfaced by the 1970s; the numbers have risen since then and are likely to continue to do so because Umar has become a significant element in the ancient struggle between Christian and Muslim scholars, propagandists, and wishful

Fig. 21. Umar ibn Said, Photograph from a Daguerreotype, 1850s or 1860s, Davidson College Library, Davidson, North Carolina.

MUSLIMS IN THE AMERICAS BEFORE COLUMBUS

by
Dr. Youssef Mroueh

- Introduction
- Historic Documents
- Geographic Explorations
- Arabic (Islamic) Inscriptions

Introduction

Numerous evidence suggests that Muslims from Spain and West Africa arrived in the Americas at least five centuries before Columbus. It is recorded, for example that in the mid-tenth century during the rule of the Umayed Caliph Abdul-Rahman III (929-961), Muslims of African origin sailed westward from the Spanish port of Delba (Palos) into the "Ocean of darkness an fog." They returned after a long absence with much booty from a "strange and curious land." It is evident that people of Muslim origin are known to have accompanied Columbus and subsequent Spanish explorers to the New World.

The last Muslim stronghold in Spain, Granada, fell to the Christians in 1492 CE, just before the Spanish inquisition was launched. To escape persecution, many non-Christians fled or embraced Catholicism. **At least two documents** imply the presence of Muslims in Spanish America before 1550 CE. Despite the fact that a decree issued in 1539 CE, by Charles V, King of Spain, forbade the grandsons of Muslims who had been burned at the stake to migrate to the West Indies. This decree was ratified in 1543 CE, and an order for the expulsion of all Muslims from overseas Spanish territories was subsequently published. Many references on the Muslim arrival in the Americas are available. They are summarized in the following notes:

Historic Documents

1. A Muslim historian and geographer Abul-Hassan Ali Ibn Al-Hussain Al-Masudi (871 - 957 CE) wrote in his book 'Muruj Adh-dhahab wa Maadin al-Jawhar' (The Meadows of Gold and Quarries of Jewels) that during the rule of the Muslim Caliph of Spain Abdullah Ibn Muhammad (888 - 912 CE), a Muslim navigator **Khashkhash Ibn Saeed Ibn Aswad** of Cordoba, Spain sailed from Delba (Palos) in 889 CE, crossed the Atlantic, reached an unknown territory (Ard Majhoola) and returned with fabulous treasures. In Al-Masudi's map of the world there is a large area in the ocean of darkness and fog (the Atlantic ocean) which he referred to as the unknown territory (the Americas).

details of his ocean journey are mentioned in Islamic references, and many Muslim scholars are aware of this recorded historical event.

3. The Muslim historian Chihab Addine Abul-Abbas Ahmad ben Fadhl **Al-Umari** (1300 - 1384 C 700 - 786 AH) described in detail the geographical explorations beyond the sea of fog and darkne of **Male's sultans** in his famous book 'Masaalik al-absaar fi Mamaalik al-amsaar (The Pathways Sights in The Provinces of Kingdoms).

4. **Sultan Mansa Kankan Musa** (1312 - 1337 CE) was the world renowned **Mandinka monarch** the West African Islamic empire of **Mali**. While traveling to Makkah on his famous Hajj in 1324 he informed the scholars of the Mamluk Bahri Sultan court (an-Nasir-eddin Muhammad III, 1309 1340 CE) in Cairo that **his brother, Sultan Abu Bakari I** (1285 - 1312 CE) had undertaken two expeditions into the Atlantic ocean. When the sultan did not return to Timbuktu from the second voyage of 1311 CE, Mansa Musa became sultan of the empire.

5. Columbus and early Spanish and Portuguese explorers were able to voyage across the Atlantic (distance of 24,000 Kilometers) thanks to Muslim geographical and navigational information, in particular maps made by Muslim traders, including Al-Masudi (871 - 957 CE) in his book **'Akhbar Az-Zaman'** (History of The World) which is based on material gathered in Africa and Asia. As a matter of fact, **Columbus had two captains of Muslim origin** during his first transatlar voyage: **Martin Alonso Pinzon** was the captain of the **Pinta**, and his brother **Vicente Yanex Pinzo** was the captain of the **Nina**. They were wealthy, expert ship outfitters who helped organize the Columbus expedition and repaired the flagship **Santa Maria**. They did this at their own expense fo both commercial and political reasons. **The Pinzon family was related to Abuzayan Muhamma III (1362 - 66 CE), the Moroccan sultan of the Marinid dynasty (1196 - 1465 CE).**

Arabic (Islamic) Inscriptions

1. Anthropologists have proven that the Mandinkas under Mansa Musa's instructions explored many parts of North America via the **Mississippi** and other rivers systems. At Four Corners, Arizona, writings show that they even brought elephants from Africa to the area.

2. Columbus admitted in his papers that on Monday, October 21, 1492 CE while his ship was sailir near **Gibara** on the north-east coast of Cuba, he saw a **mosque** on the top of a beautiful mountain. The ruins of mosques and minarets with inscriptions of Qur'anic verses have been discovered in Cuba, Mexico, Texas and Nevada.

3. **During his second voyage**, Columbus was told by the Indians of Espanola (Haiti), that Black people had been to the island before his arrival. For proof they presented Columbus with the spears of these African Muslims. These weapons were tipped with a yellow metal that the Indians called **Guanine**, a word of West African derivation meaning 'gold alloy.' Oddly enough, it is related to the Arabic world **'Ghinaa'** which means 'Wealth.' Columbus brought some Guanines back to Spain an had them tested. He learned that the metal was 18 parts gold (56.25 percent), six parts silver (18.75 percent and eight parts copper (25 percent), the same ratio as the metal produced in African metal shops of Guinea.

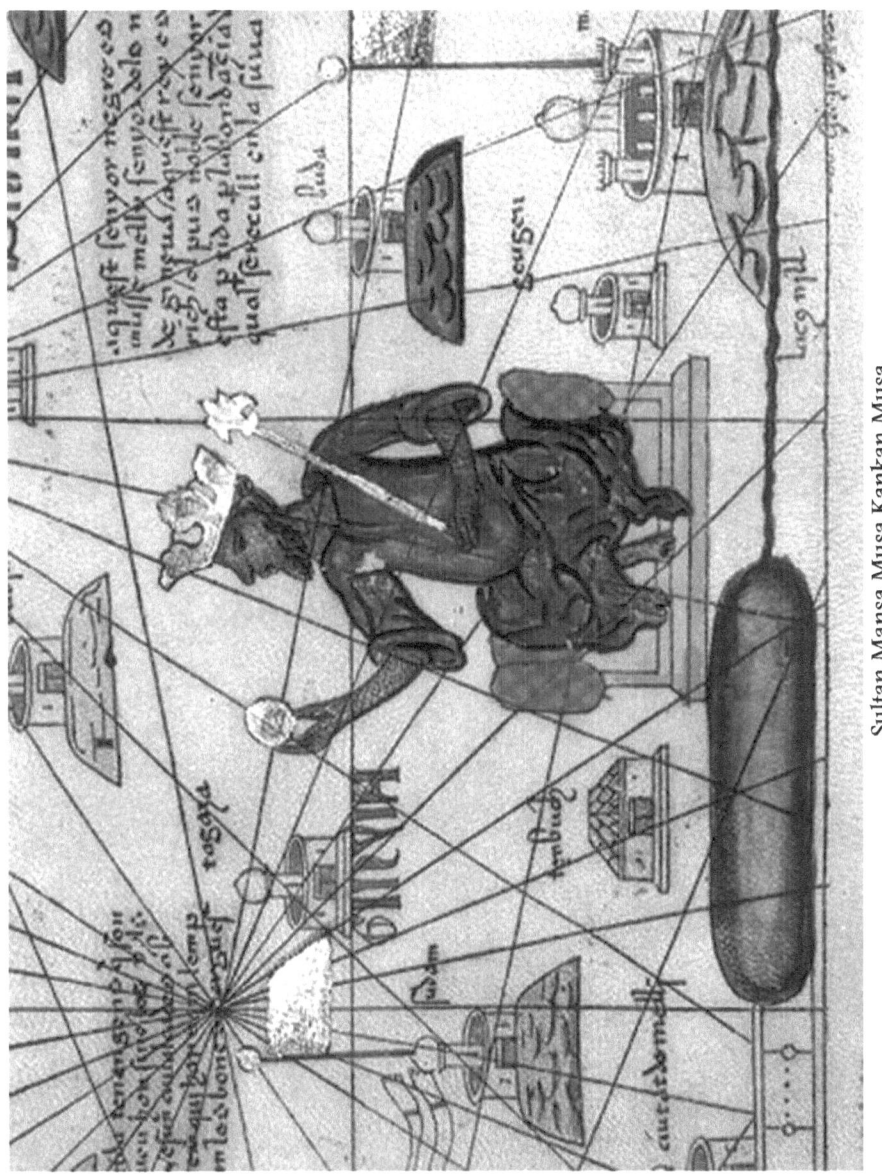

Sultan Mansa Musa Kankan Musa

Articles on Muslims in the Americas
BOOK: MUSLIM HISTORY: 570 - 1950 C.E.
BOOK: MUSLIMS IN THE INDIAN SUBCONTINENT
A Chronolgoy of Muslim History
Quotations on Islamic Civilization
Excerpts from: Islam in America

Watie served on Southern Cherokee delegation to Washington, D.C. to sign a new treaty with the United States at the end of Civil War. He died mysteriously at the age of twenty-one. (Saladin is an anglicized name for Salahuddin, the famous Muslim Sultan who liberated Jerusalem from the crusaders in 1187).

The towering redwood trees of northern California were named after Sequoyah, and his statue is displayed by the state of Oklahoma in the Statuary Hall of the national Capitol.

Allah: Allah is the proper name in Arabic for The One and Only God, The Creator and Sustainer of the universe. It is used by the Arab Christians and Jews for the God (Eloh-im in Hebrew; 'Allaha' in Aramaic, the mother tongue of Jesus). The word **Allah** (SWT) does not have a plural or gender. Allah does not have any associate or partner, and He does not beget nor was He begotten. SWT is an abbreviation of Arabic words that mean 'Glory Be To Him.'

Articles on Muslims in the Americas
BOOK: MUSLIM HISTORY: 570 - 1950 C.E.
BOOK: MUSLIMS IN THE INDIAN SUBCONTINENT
A Chronolgoy of Muslim History
Quotations on Islamic Civilization
Excerpts from: Islam in America

1828   Abdulrahman Ibrahim Ibn Sori, a former prince from West Africa and now a salve on a Georgia plantation, is freed by the order of Secretary of State Henry Clay and President John Quincy Adams. He was known to many during his lifetime as "The Prince of Slaves." A drawing of him, done by Henry Inman, is displayed in the Library of Congress. His life has also been well-documented.

1839   Sayyid Sa'id, ruler of Oman, orders his ship The Sultana to set sail for America on a trade mission. The Sultana touched port in New York, April 30, 1840. Although the voyage was not a commercial success, it marks the point of successful friendly relations between the two countries that continue to this day.

1856   The United States cavalry hire a Muslim by the name of Hajji Ali to experiment with raising camels in Arizona.

1865   The American Civil War ends. During the war, the "scorched earth" policy of the North destroyed churches, farms, schools, libraries, colleges, and a great deal of other property. The libraries at the University of Alabama managed to save one book from the debris of their library buildings. On the morning of April 4, when Federal troops reached the campus with order to destroy the university, Andre Deloffre, a modern language professor and custodian of the library, appealed to the commanding officer to spare one of the finest libraries in the South. The officer, being sympathetic, sent a courier to Gen. Croxton at his headquarters in Tuscaloosa asking permission to save the Rotunda. The general's reply was no. The officer reportedly said, "I will save one volume as a memento of this occasion. The volume selected was a rare copy of the Qur'an.

1870   The Reverend Norman, a Methodist missionary, converts to Islam.

1889	Edward W. Blyden, noted scholar and social activist, traveled throughout the eastern and southern parts of the United States, proclaiming Islam. In a speech before the Colonization Society of Chicago, Blyden told his audience that the reasons Africans choose Islam over Christianity is that, "the Qur'an protected the Black man from self-depreciation in the presence of Arabs or Europeans."
1893	Muslim immigrants from the Arab provinces of the Ottoman Empire, Syria, Lebanon, Jordan, etc. arrive in North America. They are mainly Turks, Kurds, Albanians, and Arabs.
1913	Timothy Drew (Noble Drew Ali) establishes an organization in Newark, NJ, known as the Moorish Science Temple of America (MSTA). Drew Ali reportedly was commissioned by the Sultan of Morocco to teach Islam to Negroes in the United States. The MSTA is also responsible for many of today's African-American converts to Islam.
1915	Albanian Muslims build a Masjid in Maine and establish an Islamic association. By 1919, they had established another Masjid in Connecticut. Theirs was one of the first associations for Muslims in the United States.
1920	The Red Crescent, a Muslim charity modeled after the International Red Cross, is established in Detroit.
1921	A branch of the Ahmadiyya Movement is founded in Chicago by Dr. Mufti Muhammad Sadiq. This movement converted many African Americans to Islam.
1926	Duse Muhammad Ali, mentor of Marcus Garvey and the person who had a considerable impact upon Garvey's movement, establishes an organization in Detroit known as the Universal Islamic Society. It's motto was: "One God, One Aim, One Destiny."
1926	Polish-speaking Tatars build a mosque in Brooklyn, NY which is still in use.
1930	African American Muslims establish the First Muslim Mosque in Pittsburgh, PA

1933 The Nation of Islam (NOI), one of the most significant organization sin American Muslim history, is founded. It is responsible for converting a high percentage of African Americans to Islam. It was also effective in highlighting American Christians' difficulties combating the effects of slavery and racism among African Americans. The NOI's philosophy was introduced in the United States by Fard Muhammad (Wallace Ford), a Muslim mystic who disappeared in 1933. The late Elijah Mohammed, who succeeded Fard in 1933, helped build the organization into a strong ethnic movement advocating Islam as a way of life. Two of the most famous African Americans, Muhammad Ali, and Al Hajj Malik al-Shabazz (Malcolm X), were early adherents of this movement. Both later embraced the broader multiethnic concepts of Orthodox Islam.

1934 The Lebanese Community of Cedar Rapids, Iowa, opens its first Masjid.

1939 The Islamic Mission Society is founded in New York City by Sheikh Dawood. It publishes a magazine entitled "Muslim Sunrise."

1952 Muslims in the Armed Services sue the federal government to be allowed to identify themselves as Muslims. Until then, Islam was not recognizes as a legitimate religion.

1955 The State Street Masjid in New York City is established by Sheikh Dawood Ahmed Faisal. It is still in use today and represents a special point in the development of the American Muslim community. From this Masjid was born the Dar-ul-Islam movement.

1960 The NOI's University of Islam schools flourished and drew the attention of the American media. Coverage focuses upon the Black Muslims' self-help programs for Blacks, but considered them a "threat" to the white establishment.

1962 The Dar-ul-Islam movement, another important groups among the African American Muslim community is born. Until its disappearance in 1982-1983, it made a serious impact upon the development and practice of traditional Islam in America.

1962	The newspaper Muhammad Speaks is launched. It later becomes the largest minority weekly publication in the country and reached 800,000 readers at its peak. In subsequent years, it underwent some name changes, and the NOI itself underwent various transformations. It has also been know as *Bilalian News* the *A.M. Journal* and currently, the *Muslim Journal*.
1963	The Muslim Students Association (MSA) is established as an organization to aid foreign Muslims students attending schools in the United States. MSA now has more than 100 branches nationwide. In the 1970s, it gave birth to the Islamic Medical Association (IMA), The Association of Muslim Social Scientists (AMSS), and the Association of Muslim Scientists and Engineers (AMSE).
1965	Al Hajj Malik al-Shabazz (Malcolm X) is assassinated in New York. He was one of the most outstanding Muslims in American history as well as a dedicated fighter for justice and equality for African Americans and other oppressed people.
1968	The Hanafi Movement is founded by Hamas Abdul Khaalis. The Hanafi Madh-hab Center was established in New York, but later moved to Washington DC. This movement had a membership of more than 1000 in the United States. Kareem Abdul-Jabbar a famous basketball player, is one of the Muslims who first came into contact with Islam through this movement. In 1977, Khaalis and some of his followers seized control of three District of Columbia buildings, holding hostages for more than 30 hours. One man was killed. Khaalis is now incarcerated in Washington DC, serving a sentence of 41 to 120 years. This movement marks a challenging period in American Muslim History.
1971	The Association of Muslim Scientists and Engineers is established.
1972	The Association of Muslim Scientists is launched.

1975	Elijah Muhammad, leader of the Nation of Islam, dies and is succeed by his son Warith Deen Mohammed, who has been credited with moving the NOI toward the broader universal concepts of Islam. He is now regarded as one of the leading Muslim spokesmen in the United States.
1981	The first American Islamic library is established in Plainfield, Indiana.
1982	The Islamic Society of North America (ISNA) is established in Plainfield, IN. ISNA is now an umbrella organization for many active Islamic groups seeking to further the cause of Islam in the United States.
1986	Dr. Isma'il R. Al-Faruqi and his wife are murdered in their home outside Philadelphia. Dr. and Mrs. Faruqi are the authors of the Cultural Atlas of Islam as well as many other books and research papers. Dr. Faruqi is the founder of AMSS and the International Institute of Islamic Thought, located in Northern Virginia. This truly remarkable Muslim family is responsible for some of the most constructive programs to promote Islam in the United States.
1990	Muslims hold the first solidarity conference called "Muslims Against Apartheid." This was the first conference of its kind in support of Muslims for the struggle against apartheid in South Africa. The conference was organized by the American Muslim Council.
1991	Imam Siraj Wahhaj offers an invocation (opening prayer) to the United States House of Representatives. He was the first Muslim to do so.
1991	The Muslim Members of the Military (MMM) organization hold their first "Unity in Uniform" conference. The conference took place at Bolling Air Force Base in Washington DC. According to the Untied States Department of Defense, there are more than 5000 Muslims in uniform on active duty in the military.
1991	Charles Bilal, Kountze, TX becomes the nation's first mayor in an American city.
1992	Imam Warith Deen Mohammed gives the invocation in the Senate.

OTHER MOORISH / BLACK FACTS

BLACK FACTS

INDIGENOUS BLACK AMERICANS IN THE CAROLINA'S DURING 1790 WERE CONVINCED BY BLACK MINISTERS THAT THE BEST SOLUTIONS TO AVOID CAPTIVITY OF SLAVERY WAS TO LEAVE THEIR HOMES TO RELOCATE TO THE CONTENENT OF AFRICA IN AN AREA KNOWN TODAY AS CEORLEON.

IN 1784 A BLACK MAN KNOWN AS VINCENT GUARERRO RULED MEXICO. AS THE PRESIDENT. CALIFORNIA, TEXAS, NEW MEXICO, ARIZONA, NEVADA, AND FLORIDA. DURING THIS TIME THESE STATES WERE THE NORTHERN PART OF MEXICO.

THE SEMINOLE ONE OF THE MANY INDIGENOUS BLACK TRIBES KNOWN TODAY AS BLACK INDIANS WERE THE ORIGINAL INHABITANTS OF THE STATE OF FLORIDA, MOST OF THE STATE IN THIS COUNTRY TAKE THERE NAMES FROM THE INDIGENOUS BLACK TRIBES. FOR INSTANCE ALABAMA IS NAMED AFTER THE ALI BA MU TRIBE AND MOBILE ALABAMA IS NAMED AFTER THE MU BA EL TRIBE.

NAT TURNER WHO IS KNOWN IN HISTORY TODAY AS THE MAN WHO CAUSED ONNE OF THE BIGGEST SLAVE REVOTE IN THE SOUTH. IF THE TRUTH WAS TOLD AS APOSED TO HIS STORY WE WOULD KNOW THAT NAT TURNER WAS THE LEADER OF A BLACK MILICIA OF MORE THAN 3000 MEMBERS WHO WERE ALL LAND OWNERS IN THE SOUTH.

BLACK PEOPLEN HAVE OVER 10,000 YEARS OF HISTORY IN AMERICA, FROM EGYPT TO MALI TO SOUTH AFRICA, CHINA, JAPAN, AND INDIA ALL HAVE RECORDS OF TRADE, COMMERCE AND INTERACTION WITH THE INDIGENOUS BLACK OF NORTH, SOUTH AND CENTRAL AMERICA.

CARTER G. WOODSON IS THE FOUNDER OF BLACK HISTORY MONTH HE'S ALSO THE AUTHOR OF SEVERAL BOOKS SUCH AS THE MISEDUCATION OF THE NEGRO, WHICH IS THE MOST SIGNIFICANT WORK DONE BY ANY AUTHOR PERTAINING TO THE NEGRO AN HIS KNOWLEDGE OF SELF, HE ALSO AUTHORED A VERY IMPORTANT BOOK KNOWN AS THE BLACK SLAVE OWNERS WHICH SHEDS MUCH LIGHT ON JUST HOW MISEDUCATED THE NEGRO TRULY IS.

Omari Miles El

Africans and Native Americans

THE TERM 'MOOR'

The term *moro* and its equivalents were widely used in late-medieval and early modern Europe. According to Simonet in his study of the language spoken by the Mozárabes (Christian Spaniards under Muslim rule before 1492), *mauro* meant *negro* and corresponded to Castillian usage in which *moro* was applied to horses whose color was *negro*. The corresponding *more* (French), *maurus* (Hispanic Latin), and *moro* (Valencian) were derived from Latin *morus* (*negro*) and ultimately from a Greek word meaning *oscuro*. Similarly, Mozarabic *mauro* was related to *moro* (Spanish and Italian), *mouro* (Portuguese and Gallego), *mor* (Provençal), *maure* and *more* (French), meaning 'Moro; negro; hombre de color'. These forms stemmed from Latin *maurus* (also from Greek), 'for the dark (*oscuro*) color of the *Mauritanos o' Moros* (peoples of northwest Africa)'.

The Mozarabic *maurel* and *moreno*, corresponding to Castillian, Catalan, and Portuguese *moreno* (*subniger, fuscus*, that is, less than black, darkish, *pardo*), French *moreau*, Italian *morello*, etc., were derived from Latin *morulus, morellus*, diminutives of *maurus* and *morus*.'

Finally Mozarabic *maurixco*, corresponding to Castillian *maurisco* and, later, *morisco*, stemmed from Hispanic Latin *mauriseus* for *mauricus* (*mauritano*), derived as above.

In 1591 an Italian went to Cabo Verde 'a comprar Mori per l'India Occidentali', that is, to buy African slaves (*Mori*) for the Americas.[10] To summarize, the people of northwestern Africa (Algeria, Morocco) were anciently known as Mauri or Mauritanians and this name in both Greek and

Latin came to mean 'negro' or black but also various shades of so-called 'obscure' color, i.e., darkish shades for which terms such as *fuscus*, *pardo* and *loro* were often used in later times. Moreover, derivatives such as *moreno* acquired meanings distinct from, but related to, *negro*. A 1607 dictionary states for *moreno*: 'brun, noir, obscur, couleur d'olives', quite a range.'¹¹

In any case, one can see that *mauri–more* group of terms (in various languages) did not refer to absolute black or to 'blackish' alone, but could indeed refer to a range of darker skin colors. This is also true as regards *nigri* and its forms. For example a 1494 source states that the king of Portugal possessed 'pretos de vários côres: acobreados, pretos e anegrados. . . . Habet item rex nigros varii coloris; rufos, nigros et aubnigros.'¹² Clearly the term *aubnigros* next to *nigros* indicates a variation, while *preto* (black) encompasses all of the stated colors: copperish or reddish, and so on.

An Irish Gaelic saga of the 900s (copied in 1643) states that Danish–Irish raiders attacked Spain and Mauritania in the 800s. From the latter place they 'carried off a great host of them as captives to Erin, and these are the blue men [of Erin], for Mauri is the same as black man, and Mauritania is the same as blackness. . . . Long indeed were these blue men in Erin.' The Gaelic text uses *Mauri* and *negri* and *mauritania* and *nigritudo*, obviously borrowed from Latin (the concept of 'blue men' is described in original Gaelic words).¹³

From this text we can see how the term *mauri* for *negro* spread to northern Europe and at the same time how both words could be used for shades of brown, since from our modern perspective the Mauritanians (Berbers, Moors, and others) are not regarded as being 'black' (or 'blue') in skin color. (It may be, of course, that they have become much lightened due to mixture with Romans, Spaniards, Arabs, Vandals, and so on, but some of that change in color could have preceded the 800s. Saco describers the *berberiscos* as being *fusci* (dark), *moreno*, and *aceitunado* (olive-colored) in his study of ancient slavery.)

The use of *moor* in the Dutch language will be discussed below, but here it is useful to note that the medieval Dutch understood by that term a very dark color, so that the color of coal was compared with that of a *moor*. Also it was said: 'scijnt swaert ghelike den more', he is as black as a moor.'¹⁴

The spread of *maurus* to the north can also be seen in Scotland where, in 1504–5, several references to 'More lasses' (Moor lassies) are found. At that time a child was born, referred to as 'Moris barne' (a *maurus* born). Late in 1512–13, one finds 'Elen More' and 'Blak Elene' used (one assumes) interchangeably. By 1527 'Helenor, the black moir' is referred to, while in 1567–9 there are references to 'Nageir the More.'¹⁵

...talked about, but the Moors had enslaved the Europeans before they enslaved blacks. Their women were sold like commodities into the harems and as concubines of wealthy Moors. This is the reason why the Moorish noble were for the most part bleached out, and became known as "tawny-moors", Turks and Arabs, which are no more than "fixed mulatto races". This also is the reason for the Moors in the coats of arms of noble Europeans family.

Brit-Moor Coat of Arms / Ancient Moorish Symbol of the Morocco Shrine

The so-called black nobility of Europe and the Bilderberger group. The European nations paid tribute to the Moors well into the 18th century. In the book, "United States and Barbary Powers" the English, French, Dutch, Danes, and Swedes, and I may say all nations are tributary to them." David Macritchie in the book "Ancient and Modern Britons" says that the word "Blackmail" is the result of this tribute paid to the "Black Army", or "Black Oppressors" as the English referred to them. The Moors had control of the Atlantic and the Mediterranean. This is why the Marines sing of defeating the Moors " From the halls of Montezuma (Mexico) to the shores of Tripoli", confirming in song the extent of the Moorish empire or dominions of Amexem, or Atlantis. Below is the first page

Coat of Arms

NEGROES IN COATS –OF-ARMS
OF NOBLE FAMILIES

FRANCISCAN SOCIOLOGISTS SOCIAL/POLITICAL POSITION IN AMERICA.

LOGISTICAL NOTATION:

IT IS WITHOUT DOUBT AND CLEAR THAT THE BRITISH (BRUTISH) ARE THE MOORS.....BLACK-A-MOORS. THE DRUIDS ARE THE MOORS. THE SARACENS ARE THE MOORS. THE MAGI ARE THE MOORS. THE DANES ARE THE MOORS. THE CARTHAGINIANS ARE THE MOORS. THE TORIES ARE THE MOORS., ETC. WE HAVE WELL BURIED THEIR HISTORY. THEIR PROGRESS OR CONSCIOUSNESS TO THEIR HIDDEN HERITAGE IS NOT IN THE BEST INTEREST OF ROMAN RULE. KNOWLEDGE IS POWER. IS THERE ANY MORE TO SAY?

THEY ARE NOW IN TOTAL DARKNESS (<u>BLACK</u>-NESS). KEEP THEM THERE..

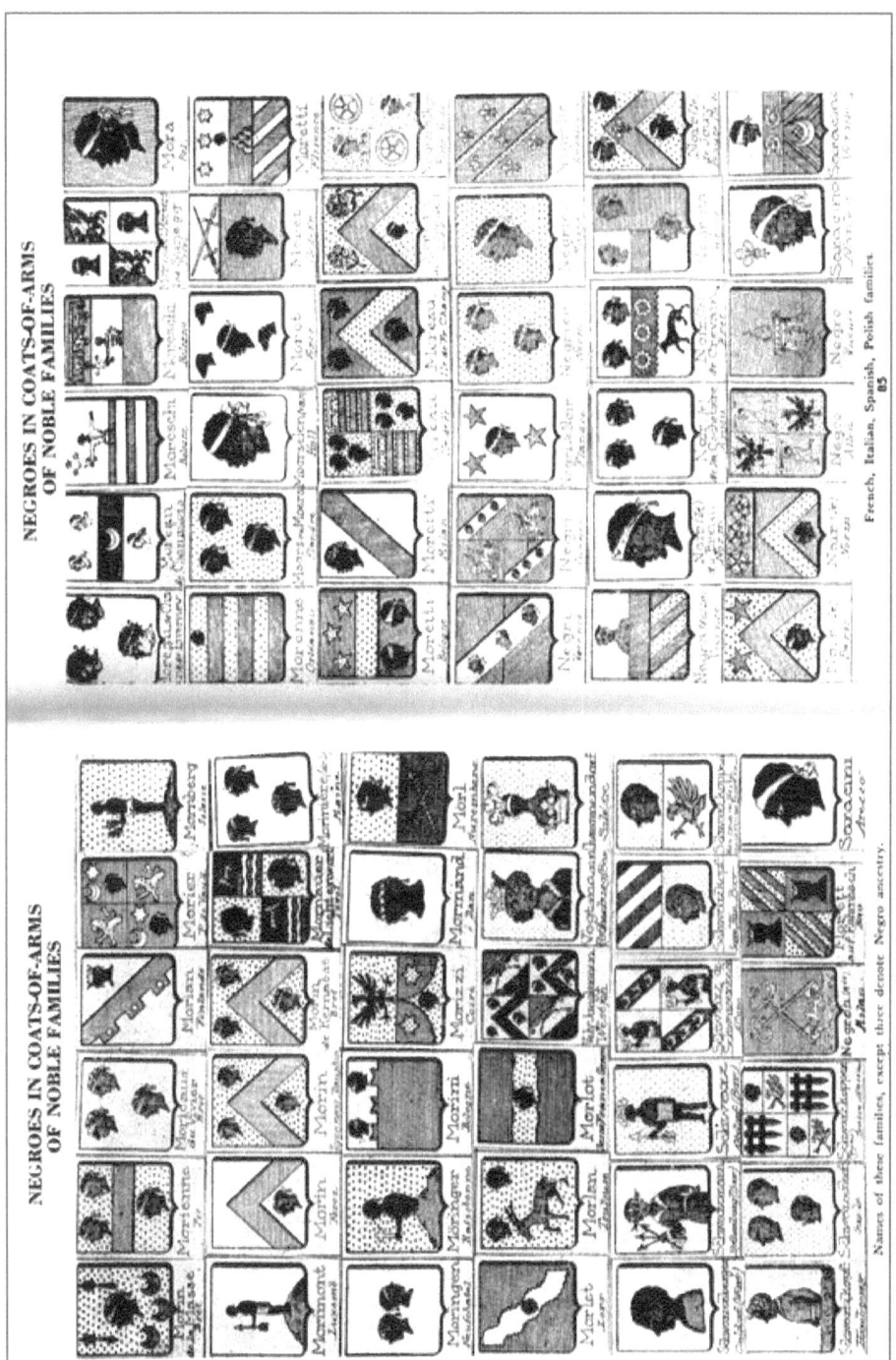

| Exploration and Settlement; Wars; Government; Civil Rights; Statistics | I | | II | Publishing; Arts and Music; Popu
Entertainment; Architecture; Thea. |

violent controversy between Anglican interests and dissenting groups, mainly Quakers and Presbyterians. Violent civil disturbances stymied enforcement of the act and the matter was soon dropped.

1705 A Virginia slavery act decreed that all imported servants were to remain in lifelong servitude. Excepted were those who had been Christians in their native country or who had been free in a Christian country. This law limited slavery to blacks and confined almost all imported blacks to slavery. An interesting exception was inserted for "Turks and Moors in amity with her majesty."

1706 An important American customhouse was built at Yorktown, Va. Yorktown had been appointed the port of entry for New York, Philadelphia, and other northern cities, though many merchants disregarded the law. Yorktown was the site of Virginia's "tea party" in 1774, when Richard Ambler, collector of revenue, led a boarding party to the *Virginia* and tossed its tea cargo overboard. The customhouse was restored in 1928.

1706 Jan. 17 Benjamin Franklin was born in Boston. His father, Josiah, a nonconformist, had fled England in 1682 and settled in New England, rearing 17 children.

1708 Aug. 30 Haverhill, Mass., was attacked and razed by the French and Indians.

1709 Sept. 3 The first major influx of Swiss and German immigrants came to the Carolinas. They had been encouraged by a grant of 13,500 acres by the proprietors to two sponsors representing German refugees from the Palatinate and Swiss emigrants from Berne.

early nineteenth century.

1705 *The History and Present State of Virginia* by Robert Beverley was published. This early accoun Virginia was popular in England and France. A r of wealth, sprung from an ancient English fam Beverley, often motivated by what he felt was an E lish misconception of the colony, painted a robust ture of plantation life.

1706 Work was begun on the Governor's Palace Williamsburg, Va., the finest residence of its time the colonies. It was not formally completed u 1720. The Governor's Palace was occupied by rc governors until the Revolutionary War, and there ter by the state governors, Patrick Henry and Thor Jefferson, until the capital was moved to Richmonc 1780.

1706 The first Latin grammar published in Amer the phenomenally popular *Accidence, A Short In duction to the Latin Tongue* by Ezekiel Cheever, w published. The book went through 20 editions, last appearing in 1785.

1706 *The Good Old Way* by Cotton Mather reflect the weakening of Puritan influence in America. In book, Mather complained that people had lost th reverence for members of the clergy and did not su port them as generously as before.

1708 A popular satirical poem by one Ebenezer Co was *The Sot-Weed Factor; or, A Voyage to Ma land,—a satire in which is described the laws, gove ment, courts, and constitution of the country, an also the buildings, feasts, frolics, entertainments, a... drunken humors of the inhabitants in that part America.* Little is known about the author.

THE ENCYCLOPEDIA OF AMERICAN FACTS & DATES

1710-1714

Settlers from European lands other than the British Isles began to come to the English colonies in large numbers. On Sept. 3, 1700, the proprietors of Carolina granted a tract of 13,500 acres to agents representing Swiss and German Palatinate emigrants. Besides wanting to better themselves economically, many of the emigrants sought religious freedom. New Bern, the second town in North Carolina, was settled in 1710 by some 650 Swiss and German colonists under the leadership of Baron Christopher de Graffenried and John Dawson. The same year 3000 Germans from the Palatinate settled near Livingston Manor, N.Y., intending to produce naval stores. They were brought to America by Robert Hunter, commissioned governor of New York and the Jerseys in 1709. The settlement was not successful and in 1713, under the leadership of Conrad Weiser, the settlers moved first to the Schoharie Valley and then to the Mohawk Valley. Eventually many of them moved

Bookselling in the colonies began before the turn the century and so was flourishing by this time. Arou 1698 Regnier Jansen, a printer in Philadelphia, was s ing books. By 1714 Andrew Bradford's Philadelphi store, the Bible and Crown, was filling orders from as away as Barbados. In 1718 John Copson sold books alc with other merchandise, a common practice. Willia Bradford, who set up in New York as a printer in 16 also ran a bookshop, as did Thomas Adams, a station after 1698. Boston, however, led the way in the bo business, with about 30 stores there by 1711. In 1724 t Boston booksellers formed an association to fix pric and otherwise regulate the trade. Boston supplied boo to all the other colonies, but its trade was especially b in New England.

1710 One of the most popular books for farmers in t American colonies was published in Boston, Ma *The Husband-Man's Guide, in Four Parts—Part firs*

Welcome!

The "Free Moors" of South Carolina

This published volume, which was originally for sale from the SCDAH, contains information dealing with the petition of the Moors. A report by the committee assigned to deal with their petition stated that they were not subject to the slave laws. There was no Act passed on this subject, however.

This manuscript was provided by the South Carolina Depart of Archives and History, Copyright ©1984, from their Research Library. This was available in book form from them, but is presently out of print. I personally thank the SCDAH for providing a copy of this record. All errors from my OCR software and proofreading are mine alone, and do not reflect on the outstanding quality of SCDAH work. FOC

The State Records of South Carolina

Journals

of the

HOUSE OF

REPRESENTATIVES, 1789-1790

MICHAEL E. STEVENS

Editor

CHRISTINE M. ALLEN

Assistant Editor

Published for the South Carolina Department of Archives and History

by the

University of South Carolina Press

Columbia, SC

8557

Copyright ©1984 by the South Carolina Department of Archives and History

First Edition

Published in Columbia, SC by the University of South Carolina Press

20 JANUARY 1790 (page) 363

(continued from previous page)

thereto, Our Committee are Mr. Hugh Rutledge, Major Pinckney & Mr. Deas.

By order of the House, Jacob Read, Speaker

Ordered That the Message be sent to the Senate and that Mr. Hugh Rutledge and Mr. Deas do carry the same.

The House proceeded to the Second reading of a Bill to Incorporate the Baptist Church on Hornes Creek in Edgefield County, State of South Carolina, when a Motion was made and Seconded that the Bill be changed into An Ordinance, which was agreed to -- the Ordinance then read through and agreed to

Ordered That the Ordinance be sent to the Senate and that Mr. Simpkins and Colonel Anderson do carry the same.

And then the House Adjourned 'til to morrow Morning 10 o'Clock.

WEDNESDAY JANUARY 20TH 1790

Read The Journals of Yesterday's proceedings.

Mr. Speaker Administered the Oath to Support the Constitution of the United States to Mr. Robert Patton, a Member of this House.

A Motion was made and Seconded, that a Message be sent to the Senate Informing them that this House propose to Ratify such Acts and Ordinances as are Engrossed, and the Great Seal of the State affixed thereto at 1 o'Clock this day, and then to Adjourn to Saturday the Twenty Seventh day of November 1790, which being agreed to, the following Message was accordingly prepared Vizt.

In the House of Representatives January 20th 1790

Honorable Gentlemen

This House propose to ratify such Acts and Ordinances as are engrossed, and the Great Seal of the State affixed thereto at 1 o'Clock this day, and then to Adjourn to Saturday the Twenty Seventh day of November next, to which this House request Your Honors Concurrence.

Ordered That the Message be signed by the Speaker, and that it be sent to the Senate and that Colonel Lushington and Mr. Drury Robertson do carry the same.

A petition was presented to the House from Sundry Free Moors, Subjects of the Emperor of Morocco; and residents in this State, praying that in case they should Commit Any Fault amenable to be brought to Justice, that they as Subjects to a Prince in Alliance with the United States of America, may be tried under the same Laws as the Citizens of this State would be liable to be tried, and not under the Negro Act, which was received and read.

[The humble Petition of Francis, Daniel, Hammond and Samuel, (Free Moors) in behalf of themselves and their wives Fatima, Flora, Sarah and

(page) 364 House Journal 4 January 1790- 20 January 1790

Clarinda, Humbly Sheweth That your Petitioners some years past had the misfortune while fighting in the defence of their Country, to be captured with their wives and made prisoners of War by one of the Kings of Africa. That a certain Captain Clark had them delivered to him on a promise that they should be redeemed by the Emperor of Morocco's Ambassador then residing in England, in order to have them returned to their own Country: *Instead of which* he brought them to this State, and sold them for slaves. Since that period they have by the greatest industry been enabled to purchase their freedom from their respective Masters: And now prayeth your Honorable House, That as free born subjects of a Prince now in Alliance with these United States; that they may not be considered as subject to a Law of this State (now in force) called the negro law: but if they should unfortunately be guilty of any crime or misdemeanor against the Laws of the Land, that they may have a just trial by a Lawful Jury. And your Petitioners as in duty bound will ever pray.][1]

Ordered That it be referred to a Committee, the following Gentlemen were accordingly appointed, Mr. Justice Grimke, General Pinckney & Mr. Edward Rutledge.

A petition was presented to the House from Sundry Inhabitants of Ninety Six District, praying that another Inspector of Tobacco for the Inspections at Campbells, Falmouth, and Adam's ferry Warehouses might be appointed, which was received and read.

Ordered That General Pinckney have leave to bring in An Ordinance agreeably to the prayer of the petitioners.

Major Pinckney from the Committee appointed to examine such Acts and Ordinances as are engrossed, and to get the great Seal of the State affixed thereto, Reported that there were Four Acts and Eight Ordinances ready for Ratifying.[2]

Mr. Isham Moore reported from the Committee to whom was referred the Petition of Richard Richardson and others, the Inhabitants of Clarendon County praying a repeal of An Act intitled "An Act to empower the Vestry and Church Wardens of the Episcopal Church of Claremont in Saint Marks Parish to sell and dispose of a Certain tract of Land in Saint Marks Parish aforesaid and for purchasing a more Convenient piece of Land as a Glebe for the Use of the Minister of the said Church of Claremont" passed March 7th 1789, which he read in his place and afterwards delivered it in at the Clerks Table where it was again read for information.

Ordered That it [be] taken into immediate Consideration, which being read through was agreed to and is as follows Vizt.

[1] Thomas Worth Claver Papers, South Caroliniana Library, University of South Carolina. This petition printed here is taken from a copy that was probably made in the nineteenth century.

[2] This report probably was made later in the day. At least one of the four acts and four of the eight ordinances were not yet engrossed at this time.

20 JANUARY 1790 (page) 373

Ordered That the Resolution be sent to the Senate for their Concurrence and that General Pinckney and Major Pinckney do carry the same.[16]

A Motion was made and Seconded that a Message be prepared and sent to the Senate requesting that they would appoint a Committee to join a Committee of this House to Contract for and inspect the printing of the Acts and Ordinances of the General Assembly passed during the present sitting—which being agreed to—A Message was prepared, which being read was agreed to and is as follows Vizt

In the House of Representatives January 20th 1790

Honorable Gentlemen

This House inform your House that this House have appointed a Committee to Contract for and Inspect the printing of the Acts and Ordinances of the General Assembly passed during the present Sitting, and to Contract with the printer now here for the printing of Three hundred Copies of the Census Act. This House request that your House would appoint a Committee to Join the Committee of this House for the said purpose. Our Committee are Mr. Speaker, Mr. Hutson, Commodore Gillon, Mr. Hugh Rutledge, Mr. Ralph Izard Junr.

Ordered That Mr. Speaker do sign the Message and that Mr. Porcher and Mr. Isham Moore do carry the same to the Senate.

The Senate returned to this House by their Clerk the following Ordinances which had been Severally read a third time in that House and passed Vizt.

An Ordinance to Incorporate a Society for the purpose of raising and Securing a Fund for the relief of the Widows and Children of the deceased Presbyterian Ministers belonging thereto, and

An Ordinance for Adding another Inspector of Tobacco for the Inspection at Campbells, Falmouth, and Adams's ferry Warehouses.

Ordered That the Ordinances be engrossed.

On Motion Resolved That the Commissioners of the Treasury be directed to pay to James Brown or to his order Fourteen pounds, for Carpenters work done for the Legislature during the present Sitting.

Ordered That the Resolution be sent to the Senate for their Concurrence and that Colonel Lushington and Mr. Ellison do carry the same.[17]

Mr. Edwd. Rutledge reported from the Committee to whom was referred the petition of the Free Moors, which he read in his place and afterwards delivered it in at the Clerks Table where it was again read for information.

Ordered That it be taken into immediate Consideration which being read through was agreed to and is as follows Viz.

Report That they have Considered the same and are of opinion that no Law of this State can in its Construction or Operation apply to them, and that persons

[16] The Senate received the resolution, but did not consider it.

[17] The Senate referred the resolution to a committee that did not report.

(page) 374 House Journal 4 January 1790-20 January 1790

who were Subjects of the Emperor of Morocco being Free in this State are not triable by the Law for the better Ordering and Governing of Negroes and other Slaves.

Resolved That this House do agree with the Report.

The Senate sent to this House by their Clerk the following message.

In the Senate January 20th 1790

Mr. Speaker & Gentlemen

This House agreeably to your request by message Just received, have appointed a Committee to Join the Committee of your House to Coi-tract for, and inspect the printing of the Acts and Ordinances of the General Assembly passed during the present Sitting, and to Contract with the printer now here for the printing Three hundred Copies of the Census Act. Our Committee are Colonel Gervais, Colonel Hampton & Mr. Brown.

By order of the Senate, D. Desaussure, President

The Senate returned to this House by their Clerk An Ordinance to Vest in Richard and Wade Hampton and their Heirs the right and property in the Bridge built across Congaree river at the place called Fridigs ferry which had been read twice in that House.[18]

The Senate returned to this House by their Clerk the following Resolutions with their Concurrence thereto Vizt.

A Resolution of the 18th instant respecting amendments to the Constitution of the United States

A Resolution of the 19th instt. respecting Tobacco Manifests

A Resolution of the 20th instant directing an Indent to be issued to Duncan Ingraham Junr.

A Resolution of the 20th instant respecting persons appointed to Public Offices, and have not taken the Oath to Support the Constitution of the United States

A Resolution of the 20th instant respecting the mode of Conducting the next General Election of Members to the Senate and House of Representatives

A Resolution of the 16th instant respecting the Debt due by this State to his most Christian Majesty

A Resolution of the 20th instant providing payment for the Pilot of GeorgeTown

A Resolution of the 20th instant respecting [an][19] Indent of James Grier Esquire

[18] This journal does not record any further consideration of the ordinance. The index to the engrossed journal states that the ordinance was withdrawn on a motion by Alexander Gillon because of a request by Wade Hampton.

[19] Journal of the House of Representatives, 1790, rough copy. The engrossed journal reads "and."

Return to The Pres Moore
American Room Records Home Page
SCGenWeb Home Page

Anyone with information in this area please contact me.

References

Courtesy of and copyright ©2000:

SC Dept. of Archives and History
8301 Parklane Road
Columbia, SC 29223

ALLAH

THE GENERAL ASSEMBLY OF PENNSYLVANIA

1933 LEGISLATIVE JOURNAL - HOUSE 5759

FILE OF THE HOUSE OF REPRESENTATIVES

RESOLUTION NO. 75

MR. WITKIN, IN PLACE - APRIL 17, 1933

MOORISH-AMERICAN SOCIETY OF PHILADELPHIA
AND USE OF THEIR NAMES

Mr. WITKIN. Mr. Speaker, I desire at this time to call up Resolution No. 75, Printer's No. 1,034. The resolution was read by the Clerk as follows:

Many sons and daughters of that proud and handsome race which inspired the architecture of Northern Africa and carried into Spain the influence of its artistic temperament have become citizens of this Nation.

In the City of Philadelphia there exists a Moorish-American Society made up of Moors who have found here the end of their quest for a home and of the children of those who journeyed here from the plains of Morocco.

This Society has done much to bring about a thorough absorption by these people of those principles, which are necessary to make them good American citizens.

These Moorish-Americans have since being here missed the use of the titles and name annexations that were so familiar at home and which are used in accordance with the doctrines of the religious faith to which they are adherents therefore be it

Resolved, That this House commends the Moorish-American Society of Philadelphia for the efficient service it has rendered the Nation in bringing about a speedy and thorough Americanization of

these former Moors and that in accordance with the fullest right of religious independence guaranteed every citizen we recognize also the right of these people to use the name affixes El or Ali or Bey or any other prefix or suffix to which they have heretofore been accustomed to use or which they may hereafter acquire the right to use.

On the question, Will the House Adopt the resolution? It was Adopted May 4, 1933

60   Next Page

Page 64 / TOC

sighted the South American continent, where some of his crew went ashore and found natives using colorful handkerchiefs of symmetrically woven cotton. Columbus noticed the these handkerchiefs resembled the head dresses and loincloths of Guinea in their colors, style and function. He referred to them as **Almayzars**. Almayzar is an Arabic word for 'wrapper,' 'cover,' 'apron' and or 'skirting,' which was the cloth the Moors (Spanish or North African Muslims) imported from West Africa (Guinea) into Morocco, Spain and Portugal.

During this voyage, Columbus was surprised that the married women wore cotton panties (bragas) and he wondered where these natives learned their modesty. **Hernando Cortez**, Spanish conqueror, described the dress of the Indian women as long veils and the dress of Indian men as 'breechcloth painted in the style of Moorish draperies.' **Ferdinand Columbus** called the native cotton garments 'breechclothes of the same design and cloth as the shawls worn by the Moorish women of Granada.' Even the similarity of the children's hammocks to those found in North Africa was uncanny.

5. **Dr. Barry Fell** (Harvard University) introduced in his book **Saga America - 1980** solid scientific evidence supporting the arrival, centuries before Columbus, of Muslims from North and West Africa. Dr. Fell discovered the existence of **Muslim schools** at Valley of Fire, Allan Springs, Logomarsino, Keyhole Canyon, Washoe and Hickison Summit Pass (Nevada), Mesa Verde (Colorado), Mimbres Valley (New Mexico) and Tipper Canoe (Indiana) dating back to **700-800 CE**. Engraved on rocks in the old western US, he found texts, diagrams and charts representing the last surviving fragments of what was once a system of schools - at both an elementary and higher levels. The language of instruction was North African Arabic written with **old Kufic Arabic script**. The subjects of instruction included writing, reading, arithmetic, religion, history, geography, mathematics, astronomy and sea navigation.

The **descendants** of the Muslim visitors of North America are members of the present Iroquois, Algonquin, Anasazi, Hohokam and Olmec native people.

6. There are **565 names of places** (villages, towns, cities, mountains, lakes, rivers, etc.) in USA (484) and Canada (81) which are derived from Islamic and Arabic roots. These places were originally named by the natives in **pre-Columbian period**. Some of these names carried holy meanings such as: **Mecca** (Indiana) - 720 inhabitants, **Makkah** Indian tribe (Washington), **Medina** (Idaho) - 2100, Medina (NY) - 8500, Medina and Hazen (North Dakota) - 1100 and 5000, respectively, Medina (Ohio) - 12,000, Medina (Tennessee) - 1100, Medina (Texas) - 26,000, Medina (Ontario) -1200, **Mahomet** (Illinois) - 3200, Mona (Utah) - 1100, Arva (Ontario) - 700, and many others. A careful study of the **names of the native Indian tribes** revealed that many names are derived from Arab and Islamic roots and origins, i.e. Anasazi, Apache, Arawak, Arikana, Chavin Cherokee, Cree, Hohokam, Hupa, Hopi, Makkah, Mahigan, Mohawk, Nazca, Zulu, Zuni, etc.

Based on the above historical, geographical and linguistic evidence, a call to celebrate the millennium of the Muslim arrival to the Americas (996-1996), five centuries before Columbus, has been issued to all Muslim nations and communities around the world. We hope that this call will receive complete understanding and attract enough support.

Webster's Third New International Dictionary

OF THE ENGLISH LANGUAGE
UNABRIDGED

A Merriam-Webster
REG. U.S. PAT. OFF.

Utilizing all the experience and resources of more than one hundred years of Merriam-Webster dictionaries

EDITOR IN CHIEF
PHILIP BABCOCK GOVE, Ph.D.
AND
THE MERRIAM-WEBSTER
EDITORIAL STAFF

G. & C. MERRIAM COMPANY, *Publishers*
SPRINGFIELD · MASSACHUSETTS · U.S.A.

AN AMERICAN DICTIONARY

OF THE

ENGLISH LANGUAGE;

CONTAINING

THE WHOLE VOCABULARY OF THE FIRST EDITION IN TWO VOLUMES QUARTO; THE ENTIRE CORRECTIONS
AND IMPROVEMENTS OF THE SECOND EDITION IN TWO VOLUMES ROYAL OCTAVO;

TO WHICH IS PREFIXED

AN INTRODUCTORY DISSERTATION

ON THE ORIGIN, HISTORY, AND CONNECTION, OF THE LANGUAGES OF WESTERN ASIA AND EUROPE, WITH
AN EXPLANATION OF THE PRINCIPLES ON WHICH LANGUAGES ARE FORMED.

BY NOAH WEBSTER, LL.D.,

Member of the American Philosophical Society in Philadelphia; Fellow of the American Academy of Arts and Sciences in Massachusetts;
Member of the Connecticut Academy of Arts and Sciences; Fellow of the Royal Society of Northern Antiquaries in Copenhagen;
Member of the Connecticut Historical Society; Corresponding Member of the Historical Societies in Massachusetts,
New York, and Georgia; of the Academy of Medicine in Philadelphia, and of the Columbian Institute
in Washington; and Honorary Member of the Michigan Historical Society.

GENERAL SUBJECTS OF THIS WORK.

I.—ETYMOLOGIES OF ENGLISH WORDS, DEDUCED FROM AN EXAMINATION AND COMPARISON OF WORDS OF CORRESPONDING ELE-
MENTS IN TWENTY LANGUAGES OF ASIA AND EUROPE.
II.—THE TRUE ORTHOGRAPHY OF WORDS, AS CORRECTED BY THEIR ETYMOLOGIES.
III.—PRONUNCIATION EXHIBITED AND MADE OBVIOUS BY THE DIVISION OF WORDS INTO SYLLABLES, BY ACCENTUA
MARKING THE SOUNDS OF THE ACCENTED VOWELS, WHEN NECESSARY, OR BY GENERAL RULES.
IV.—ACCURATE AND DISCRIMINATING DEFINITIONS, ILLUSTRATED, WHEN DOUBTFUL OR OBSCURE, BY EXAMPLES OF T
SELECTED FROM RESPECTABLE AUTHORS, OR BY FAMILIAR PHRASES OF UNDISPUTED AUTHORITY.

REVISED AND ENLARGED,

BY CHAUNCEY A. GOODRICH,

PROFESSOR IN YALE COLLEGE.

WITH PRONOUNCING VOCABULARIES OF SCRIPTURE, CLASSICAL, AND GEOGRAPHICAL NAMES.

TO WHICH ARE NOW ADDED

PICTORIAL ILLUSTRATIONS,

TABLE OF SYNONYMS, PECULIAR USE OF WORDS AND TERMS IN THE BIBLE, APPENDIX OF NEW
PRONOUNCING TABLE OF NAMES OF DISTINGUISHED PERSONS, ABBREVIATIONS, LAT
FRENCH, ITALIAN, AND SPANISH PHRASES, ETC.

228576

SPRINGFIELD, MAS
PUBLISHED BY GEORGE AND CHAE
CORNER OF MAIN AND STATE ST
1859.

A-MER'I-CAN, *a.* Pertaining to America.

A-MER'I-CAN, *n.* A native of America; originally applied to the aboriginals, or copper-colored races, found here by the Europeans; but now applied to the descendants of Europeans born in America, especially to the inhabitants of the United States

The name American must always exalt the pride of patriotism.
— *Washington.*

moorland

²moor \"\ n -s usu cap [ME More, fr. MF, fr. L Maurus, prob. of Berber origin] 1 a : a member of a dark-skinned people of mixed Arab and Berber ancestry inhabiting ancient Mauretania in No. Africa and conquering Spain in the 8th century A.D. : MOROCCAN   b : BERBER   2 : MUSLIM; esp : ¹MOORMAN — compare MORO   3 a archaic : BLACKAMOOR   b : one of a group of people of mixed Indian, white, and Negro ancestry in central Delaware — compare NANTICOKE   4 : a goldfish similar to the fringetail but velvety black

BEY, (bā,) n. In the *Turkish dominions*, a governor of a town or particular district of country; also, in some places, a prince; the same as Beg. [See Beg.] *Eton.*

DEY, (dā,) *n.* A Turkish title of dignity given to the governor of Algiers before the French conquest.

— BLACK

BLACK, a. [Sax. *blac*, and *blæc*, black, pale, wan, livid; *blacian*, *blæcan*, to become pale, to turn white, to become black, to blacken; *blæc*, ink; Sw. *blek*, pale, wan, livid; *bleck*, ink; *bloka*, to insolate, to expose to the sun, or to bleach; also to lighten, to flash; D. *bleek*, pale; *bleeken*, to bleach; G. *bleich*, pale, wan, bleak; *bleichen*, to bleach; Dan. *blæk*, ink; *bleeg*, pale, wan, bleak, sallow; *blege*, to bleach. It is remarkable that *black*, *bleak*, and *bleach*, are all radically one word. The primary sense seems to be, pale, wan, or sallow, from which has proceeded the present variety of significations.]

BLACK, v. t. To make black; to blacken; to soil. *Boyle.*

BLACK'-ACT, n. [*black* and *act*.] The English statute 9 Geo. I., which makes it felony to appear armed in any park or warren, &c., or to hunt or steal deer, &c., with the face *blacked* or disguised. *Blackstone.*

BLACK'-ART, n. Conjuration.

BLACK'A-MOOR, n. [*black* and *moor*.] A negro; a black man

NE'GRO, *n.* [It. and Sp. *negro*, black, from L. *niger*.] A native or descendant of the black race of men in Africa. The word is never applied to the tawny or olive-colored inhabitants of the northern coast of Africa, but to the more southern race of men who are quite black.

AL'BI-NISM, n. The state or condition of an albino.
AL-BI'NO, n. [L. albus, white.]
A white person belonging to a race of [negroes?]
This term was originally applied, by the Portu[guese]
to the white negroes on the coast of Africa;
now applied generally to denote individuals [of a]
race of men, characterized by a preternatural [white-]
ness of the skin and hair, and a peculiar red[ness of]
the iris and pupil of the eye.   P. [Cyc.]
AL-BI'NO-ISM, n. The state of an albino.
                                        Parting[ton.]
AL'BI-ON, n. An ancient name of England
used in poetry. It is supposed this name was [given]
to it on account of its white cliffs.

Copied from the Walker English Dictionary Printed in 1828

MOOR, mōōr. s. 311 A marsh, a fen, a bog, a tract of low and watery ground; a negro, a black-a-moor.

NEG — NER

chanter; a conjuror; one who by charms can converse with the ghosts of the dead.
NECROMANCY, něk'rō-măn-sě. s. 519. The art of revealing future events, by communication with the dead; enchantment, conjuration.
NECTAR, něk'tŭr. s. 88. The supposed drink of the heathen gods.
NECTARED, něk'tŭrd. a. 88. Tinged with nectar.
NECTAREOUS, něk-tā'rē-ŭs. a. Resembling nectar, sweet as nectar.
NECTARINE, něk'tŭr-ĭn. s. 150. Sweet as nectar.
NECTARINE, něk'tŭr-ĭn. s. 150. A fruit of the plum kind. This fruit differs from a peach in having a smooth rind and the flesh firmer.
NEED, nēēd. s. 246. Exigency, pressing difficulty, necessary; want, distressed poverty; lack of any thing for use.
To NEED, nēēd. v. a. To want, to lack.
To NEED, nēēd. v. n. To be wanted, to be necessary, to have necessity of any thing.
NEEDER, nēēd'ŭr. s. 98. One that wants any thing.
NEEDFUL, nēēd'fŭl. a. Necessary, indispensably requisite.
NEEDFULLY, nēēd'fŭl-lē. ad. Necessarily.
NEEDFULNESS, nēēd'fŭl-nĕs. s. Necessity.
NEEDILY, nēēd'ĕ-lē. ad. In poverty, poorly.
NEEDINESS, nēēd'ē-nĕs. s. Want, poverty.
NEEDLE, nēē'dl. s. 405. A small instrument pointed at one end to pierce cloth, and perforated at the other to receive the thread; the small steel bar which in the mariner's compass

NEGLECTION, nĕg-lĕk'shŭn. s. The state of being negligent.
NEGLECTFULLY, nĕg-lĕkt'fŭl-lē. ad. With heedless inattention.
NEGLECTIVE, nĕg-lĕk'tĭv. a. 512. Inattentive to, or regardless of.
NEGLIGENCE, nĕg'lē-jĕnse. s. Habit of omitting by heedlessness, or of acting carelessly.
NEGLIGENT, nĕg'lē-jĕnt. a. Careless, heedless, habitually inattentive.
NEGLIGENTLY, nĕg'lē-jĕnt-lē. ad. Carelessly, heedlessly, without exactness.
To NEGOTIATE, nē-gō'shē-āte. v. n. 542. To have intercourse of business, to traffick, to treat.
NEGOTIATION, nē-gō-shē-ā'shŭn. s. Treaty of business.
NEGOTIATOR, nē-gō'shē-ā-tŭr. s. 521. One employed to treat with others.
NEGOTIATING, nē-gō'shē-ā-tĭng. a. 410. Employed in negotiation.
NEGRO, nē'grō. s. A blackmoor.
☞ Some speakers, but those of the very lowest order, pronounce this word as if written ne-ger.
To NEIGH, nā. v. n. 249. To utter the voice of a horse.
NEIGH, nā. s. The voice of a horse.
NEIGHBOUR, nā'bŭr. s. 249 One who lives near to another; one who lives in familiarity with another; any thing near or near; intimate, confidant; in divinity, one partaking of the same nature, and therefore entitled to good offices.
☞ For what I apprehend to be the genuine sound of the diphthong in the first syllable of this word, see Eight.

NEGRO, nē'grō. s. A blackmoor.
☞ Some speakers, but those of the very lowest order, pronounce this word as if written ne-ger.

without need.
NEEDLESSNESS, nēēd'lĕs-nĕs. s. Unnecessariness.
NEEDLESS, nēēd'lĕs. a. Unnecessary, not requisite.
NEEDMENT, nēēd'mĕnt. s. Something necessary. Obsolete.
NEEDS, nēēdz. ad. Necessarily, by compulsion, indispensably.
NEEDY, nēēd'ē. a. Poor, necessitous.
NE'ER, nāre. 97, 247. A poetical contraction for never.
To NEESE, nēēze. v. n. To sneeze. Obsolete.
NEF, něf. s. The body of a church.
NEFARIOUS, nē-fā'rē-ŭs. a. Wicked, abominable.
NEGATION, nē-gā'shŭn. s. Denial, the contrary to affirmation; description by negative.
NEGATIVE, nĕg'gă-tĭv. a. 157. Denying, contrary to affirmative; implying only the absence of something; having the power to withhold, though not to compel.
NEGATIVE, nĕg'gă-tĭv. s. A proposition by which something is denied; a particle of denial, as, Not.
NEGATIVELY, nĕg'gă-tĭv-lē. ad. With denial, in the form of denial, not affirmatively; in form of speech implying the absence of something.
To NEGLECT, nĕg-lĕkt'. v. a. To omit by carelessness; to treat with scornful heedlessness; to postpone.
NEGLECT, nĕg-lĕkt'. s. Instance of inattention; careless treatment; negligence, frequency of neglect; state of being unregarded.
NEGLECTER, nĕg-lĕk'tŭr. s. 98. One who neglects.
NEGLECTFUL, nĕg-lĕkt'fŭl. a. Heedless, careless, inattentive; treating with indifference

NEITHER, nē'ṯẖŭr. conjunction.
A particle used in the first branch of a negative sentence, and answered by Nor; as, Fight Neither with small Nor great. It is sometimes in the second branch of a negative or prohibition to any sentence: as, Ye shall not eat of it, Neither shall ye touch it.
NEITHER, nē'ṯẖŭr. pron. 98. Not either, not one nor other.
NEOPHYTE, nē'ō-fīte. s. 156. One regenerated, a convert.
NEOTERICK, nē-ō-tĕr'ĭk. a. 509. Modern, novel, late.
NEPENTHE, nē-pĕn'ṯẖē. s. A drug that drives away all pains.
NEPHEW, nĕv'vū. s. The son of a brother or sister.
NEPHRITICK, nē-frĭt'ĭk. a. 509. Belonging to the organs of urine; troubled with the stone; good against the stone.
NEPOTISM, nĕp'ō-tĭzm. s. Fondness for nephews.
☞ I have differed from all our orthoepists in the pronunciation of this word, by making the first syllable short; not because there is no et in the Latin Nepos, but because the antepenultimate accent of our own language, when not followed by a diphthong, naturally shortens the vowel it falls upon. 535.
NERVE, nĕrv. s. The nerves are the organs of sensation passing from the brain to all parts of the body; it is used by the poets for sinew or tendon.
NERVELESS, nĕrv'lĕs. a. Without strength.
NERVOUS, nĕr'vŭs. a. 314. Well strung, strong, vigorous; relating to the nerves; having weak or diseased nerves.
NERVY, nĕr'vē. a. Strong, vigorous.

Salvation   Allah   Unity

The Moorish Science Temple
of America
THE DIVINE CONSTITUTION AND BY-LAWS

Act 1: The Grand Sheik and the chairman of the Moorish Science Temple of America is in power to make law and enforce laws with the assistance of the Prophet and the Grand Body of the Moorish Science Temple of America. The Assistant Grand Sheik is to assist the Grand Sheik in all affairs if he lives according to Love, Truth, Peace, Freedom, and Justice, and it is known before the members of the Moorish Science Temple of America.

Act 2: All meetings are to be opened and closed promptly according to the Circle Seven and Love, Truth, Peace, Freedom, and Justice. Friday is our Holy Day of rest, because on a Friday the first man was formed in flesh and on a Friday the first man departed out of flesh and ascended unto his father God, Allah, for that cause Friday is the Holy Day for all Moslems all over the world.

Act 3: Love, Truth, Peace, Freedom, and Justice must be proclaimed and practiced by all members of the Moorish Science Temple of America. No member is to put in danger or accuse falsely his brother or sister on any occasion at all that may harm his brother or sister, because Allah is Love.

Act 4: All members must preserve these Holy and Divine laws, and all members must obey the laws of the government, because by being a Moorish American, you are a part and parcel of the government, and must live the life accordingly.

Act 5: This organization of the Moorish Science Temple of America is not to cause any confusion or to overthrow the laws and constitution of the said government but to obey hereby.

Act 6: With us all members must proclaim their nationality and we are teaching our people their nationality and their divine creed that they may know that they are a part and a parcel of this said government, and know that they are not Negroes, Colored Folks, Black People, or Ethiopians, because these names were given to slaves by slave holders in 1779 and lasted until 1865 during the time of slavery, but this is a new era of time now, and all men now must proclaim their free national name to be recognized by the government in which they live and the nations of the earth, this is the reason why Allah the Great God of the universe ordained Noble Drew Ali, the Prophet to redeem his people from their sinful ways. The Moorish Americans are the descendants of the ancient Moabites whom inhabited the North Western and South Western shores of Africa.

Act 7: All members must promptly attend their meetings and become a part and a parcel of all uplifting acts of the Moorish Science Temple of America. Members must pay their dues and keep in line with all necessities of the Moorish Science Temple of America, then you are entitled to the name of "Faithful." Husband, you must support your wife and children; wife, you must obey your husband and take care of your children and look after the duties of your household. Sons and daughters must obey father and mother and be industrious and become a part of the uplifting of fallen humanity. All Moorish Americans must keep their hearts and minds pure with love, and their bodies clean with water. This Divine Covenant is from your Holy Prophet Noble Drew Ali, through the guidance of his Father God Allah.

Noble Drew Ali
Founder

MOORISH AMERICAN PRAYER

Allah the Father of the universe, the Father of Love, Truth, Peace, Freedom and Justice. Allah is my protector, my guide, and my salvation by night and by day, through his Holy Prophet Drew Ali. "Amen."

THE MOORISH SCIENCE TEMPLE OF AMERICA

Home Office: 37th & Federal St.   Chicago, Il, U.S.A.

The Great Meeting Is One

A Warning from the Prophet
The Young Men Moorish National
Business League

NOBLE DREW ALI, *FOUNDER*

OF

MOORISH SCIENCE TEMPLE OF AMERICAN, INC.

BALTIMORE, MARYLAND

The citizens of all free National Government according to their National Constitutions are of all one family bearing one free National name. Those who fail to recognize the free National name of their Constitutional Government are classed as undesirable and are subject to all inferior names, abuses and mistreatment that the citizens care to bestow upon them and it is a sin for any group of people to violate the National Constitutional Laws of a free National Government and to cling to the names and principals that delude to slavery.

I, the Prophet was prepared by the Great God Allah to warn my people to repent from their sinful ways and to go back to the state of mind to their forefathers' Divine and National Principles that they will be law abided and receive their divine rights as citizens according to the free National Constitution that was prepared for all free National beings—they are to claim their own free National name and religion.

There is but one issue, for them to be recognized by this Government and of the earth and that comes only through the connection of the Moorish Divine National Movement which is incorporated in this Government and recognized by all other Nations of the World. And through it they and their children can receive their divine rights, unmolested by other citizens.

They can cast a free National Ballot to the polls under the free National Constitution of the United States Government and not under a "Granted Privilege" as has been the existing condition for many generations.

You who doubt whether I, the Prophet and my principles are right for the redemption of my people, go to those that know law, in the City Hall and among the officials in your government and ask them under intelligent tone and they will be glad to render you a favorable reply, for they are glad to see me bring you out of the darkness into light.

Money doesn't make the man, it is free National standards and power that makes a man and a nation. The wealth of all National Governments gold, silver and commerce belongs to the citizens alone and without your National Citizenship by name and principle, you have no true wealth. I am hereby calling on all true citizens that stands for a National Free government and the enforcement of the Constitution, to help me in my great missionary work. I need support from all true American Citizens of the United States of America to help me save my people who have fallen from the Constitutional laws of this government. I am depending on your support to get them back to the constitutional fold again, that they may learn to LOVE instead of HATE and will live according to Love, Truth, Peace, Freedom and Justice, supporting our free National Constitution of the United States of America.

- 2-

I love my people and I desire their Unity and Mine back to their own free National and Divine Standard, because day by day they have been violating the National and Constitutional laws of their government by claiming names and principles that are unconstitutional. If Italians, Greeks, English, Chinese, Japanese, Turks and Arabians are forced to proclaim their free national name and religion before the constitutional government of the United States of America, it is no more than right that the law be forced upon all American citizens alike. In all other governments when a man is born and reared there and asked his name and national descent and fails to give it, he is misused, imprisoned, or exiled. Any group of people that fails to answer up to the Constitutional Standards of law by name and principle because to be a citizen of any government, you must claim your National name descent; because they place their trust upon issue and names that they are not a part and partial of, and neither were they formed by their forefathers. The word

Negro deludes in the Latin language to the word "nigger" the same as the word "colored" deludes to anything that is painted, varnished, or dyed. Every nation must bear a national descent name of their forefathers because honoring they fathers and they mothers your days will be lengthened upon this earth. These names have never been recognized by a true American citizen of this day.

Through your free National name you are known and are recognized by all nations of the earth that are recognized by said National Government in which they live. The 14th and 15th amendments brought the north and south in unit placing the southerner which was at that time without power with the Constitutional Body of power; and at that time 1865, the free National Constitutional law that was enforced since 1774 declared all men equal and free and if all men are declared by the free National Constitution to be free and equal, since that constitution has never been changed there is no need for the application of the 14th and 15th amendment for the salvation of our people and citizens.

So there isn't but one supreme issue for my people to use to redeem that which was lost and that is through the above statements. Then the lion and the lamb can lie down together in yonder hills and neither will be harmed, because Love, Truth, Peace, Freedom and Justice will be ranging in this land in those days the United States will be one of the greatest civilized and prosperous government of the world, but if the above principles are not carried out by the citizens and my people in this government, the worse is yet to come, because the Great God of the Universe is not pleased with the works that are being performed in North America by my people and this great sin must be removed from the land to save it from enormous earth quakes, diseases, etc.

And I, the Prophet do hereby believe that this administration of the government being more wisely prepared by more genius citizens that believe in their free National Constitution and laws, and through the helps of such class of citizens, I, the Prophet, truly believe that my people will find the true and divine way of their forefathers and learn to stop serving carnal customs and merely ideas of man, that has never done them any good, but has always harmed them. -3-

So I, the Prophet, is hereby calling aloud with a divine plea to all true

American citizens to help me remove this great sin which has been committed and is being practiced by my people in the United States of America; because they know it is not the true and divine way and without understanding they have fallen from the true light into utter darkness of sine and there is not a nation on earth today that will recognize them socially, religiously, politically, and educationally, etc. in their present conditions of endeavorment in which they themselves try to force on a civilized world, they will not refrain from their sinful way of action and their deeds have brought "Jim-Crowism", "segregation" and everything that brings harm to human beings on earth. They fought the southerner for all these great misuses, but I have traveled in the south and have examined conditions there, and it is the works of my people continuously practicing the things which bring dishonor, disgrace, and disrespect to any nation that lives the life. And I am hereby calling on all true American citizens for moral support and finance to help me in my great missionary work to bring my people out of darkness into marvelous light.

FROM THE PROPHET

Noble Drew Ali

1928 C.E. – 1933 C.E.
The U.S.: Bankruptcy And The Moors

The purveyors of so-called white supremacy were just walking along minding their own business; suppressing, destroying, and/or misrepresenting the truth about history... Moor's history in particular when out of no where came the savior for the fallen people that they had extinguished the light and life within. His appellation is Noble: Drew-Ali.

Having traveled the world, Noble: Drew-Ali obtained knowledge, wisdom, understanding, and over-standing into the many truths the oppressors were working so hard to hide. After detecting our true identity as Moors and our true history as possessors of the oldest artifacts and burial sites in what has been misnomered as the so-called "Americas" as opposed to the lies the so-called white supremist was spewing forth [All "blacks" were brought to the "Americas" by us to be our slaves]; Noble: Drew-Ali implemented a series of actions to begin the process of resurrecting our people from the comatose and dead levels. These efforts culminated in the re-emergence of the Moors as a community in the sense of a body-politic that was gestating/rebuilding into a nation once again.

In 1928 C.E., the Pan-American-Conference was held in Havana, Cuba. Secretary Of State Hughes went down to represent the United:States and Noble: Drew-Ali went down to represent the Moors. At that conference, the mandate for the land mass of Greater-Amexem [North, Central, and South-Central-Amexem] misnomered as the North, Central, and South "Americas" was returned to the Moors. Noble: Drew-Ali knew what this meant and what the ramifications of this was and is. Several stop gap measures were taken by Noble: Drew-Ali to secure our [The Moors] birthright inheritance and beneficiary interest as Moors to the land mass within the aforementioned land mandate. The actions of Noble: Drew-Ali were detected by the so-called white-supemists and they immediately proceeded to act to do all they could to impede his work and take him out.

Fortunately natural law governs all events thus by the time the oppressor made his move on Noble: Drew-Ali, Noble: Drew-Ali had already put things in motion. This scared the international banksters because land and labor is where all of your wealth comes from in the carnal world and Noble: Drew-Ali had just yanked all the land from so-called "Alaska" to so-called "Argentina" out from under them. Even though we, the Moors as a community were mentally comatose at that time the international banksters recognized that the potential for our instant return to our place of prominence on the global scene existed. Thus the international banksters recalled all of their loans in a panic which in turn put a squeeze on their stock market which caused its collapse 2 months after the assassination of Noble: Drew-Ali.

Nevertheless the so-called European on both sides of the Atlantic knew that their system was and is existing and functioning on borrowed time. They also realize that the length of that borrowed time is directly tied to the length of our [The Moors] ignorance/lack of knowledge of our self, our history, our culture, and what is rightly/justly ours. This fact is what has compelled the so-called white supremist to do all that is possible to keep the undeclared/mentally-comatose-Moors from ever waking up and

http://www.radiostationcentral.com/DOCUMENTS/drewali.htm   5/22/2001 reclaiming all that rightly belongs to our people and at the same time; keep the rank and file unsuspecting so-called "Europeans" from finding out what is really going on.

Noble: Drew-Ali's works as a result of what transpired at the Pan-American: Conference touched off a flurry of activity on both sides of the Atlantic because the so-called "European" from both sides of the Atlantic knew what was coming as a result. The actions of Noble: Drew-Ali caused the so-called "Europeans" to assemble themselves to conspire and plot a way to deal with what they thought would be the re-emergence of the Moors to whom their respective countries are tributary to as they always have been [The U.S. And Barbary Powers by David Macritchie written in the 1800's C.E. documents this fact].

Noble: Drew-Ali knew that the time of our [The Moors] resurrection had not come and knew that his days were numbered. In fact, Noble: Drew-Ali stated " It will take you Moors 50 years to figure out what I have done. What I have done is not for you Moors but for the 3rd and 4th generation from now. There will be new Moors that will come with their eyes open seeing and knowing and they will set you old Moors in the back and carry out my law". The so-called "European" was horrified at the potential of our people rising 71 years ago yet Noble: Drew-Ali knew our minds were not ready then.

Nevertheless the so-called United:States, Great-Britain, France, Germany, Italy, Spain, and Portugal convened in Geneva, Switzerland for 5 continuous years [1928 C.E.-1932 C.E.] to set up what would be the policy of all of the participating countries. These 5 years of meetings became known as the Geneva-Convention. In 1930 C.E., the so-called United:States, Great-Britain, France, Germany, Italy, Spain, and Portugal all declared bankruptcy. Any attempt to obtain the minutes of the 1930 C.E. Geneva-Convention are futile because they publish the volumes of minutes for every year of the Geneva conventions including 1930 C.E. but refuse to make the 1930 C.E. minutes available to the public because they contain the evidence of the bankruptcy.

Going into 1932 C.E., the aforementioned states stopped meeting in Geneva. In 1932 C.E. Franklin-Roosevelt became the U.S.: President and his job was to put into place and administer the bankruptcy that the United:States had declared 2 years earlier and hide the bankruptcy from the unsuspecting public by establishing a re-organization plan [The New Deal/Administrative State that functions under the "color" of the United States of America]. The United States of America and the United States for America along with the United-States: Constitution became defunct from that moment on and all that remained was the insolvent/bankrupt for profit corporation known as the United:States/UNITED STATES[Codified and documented in Title 26 of the Code of Federal Regulations section 1.911-2(h), In Re Merriam 36 NE 505. 141 N.Y. 479 upheld by the 16 S. Ct 1073. 163 U.S. 625 41 L.Ed 287 See also 16 Stat 419 and District-Of-Columbia-v-Cluss 103 U.S. 705.26-1 Ed.455] operating a democratic military venue

under martial law [War Powers Act] and the Uniform-Commercial-Code [Hebrew Commercial Law].

The so called "States" all revamped their local constitutions by 1938 C.E. to take into account their capitulation to the bankrupt mother corporation doing business as the United:States thus clearing the way for the Buck Act of 1940 allowing the corporate United:States to extend its jurisdiction and by default usurp all sovereignty over the now defunct State-Republics.

Getting back to Roosevelt, he was sworn into the United-States: Presidency in January 1933 C.E. and wasted no time getting started with the bankruptcy. Roosevelt immediately shut the banks down [Banking Holiday] and proceeded to pull all of the gold out of circulation while replacing it with a debt currency/tender/i.o.u. with the Moors' seal [The pyramid with the all seeing eye] on the back of the U.S.: 1 dollar bill/federal reserve note.

The Clock of Destiny Book II by C.M.: Bey on page 6 states " The Amazon red skin white moors' progress was guided by the cycle of the planets Jupiter and Mars from 1789 C.E. to 1933 C.E., a period of 140 years. Mars passes through the 12 signs of the zodiac 72 times and Jupiter passes through the 12 signs of the zodiac 12 signs in a 140 years. Thus from 1789 C.E. to 1933 C.E. spelled the rise and fall of Rome on a universal scale [Take note of the Fasci symbols on both sides of the speakers podium in the U.S.: Congress]. Keeping in mind that the first 8 presidents were Moors and they were in power from 1776 C.E. to 1789 C.E. when the keys of power were transferred into the custodianship of the Mystic Turks [So-called "European" Masons] and Shriners that the Moors charged with the duty and responsibility of protecting our sacred shrine [New-Jerusalem/Washington, D.C.] and our sciences until we as a people arose from our state of spiritual, moral and ethical decay and awaken from our slumber to reclaim all that rightfully belongs to us from their custodianship.

The 9th U.S.: President, George-Washington was a Grand Master Mason under the tutorage of Emmanuel-Mu-Ali-Ben: Bey [Benjamin-Banneker]. George-Washington was the first and U.S.: President and Grand Master Mason Franklin Roosevelt was the last so-called "European" President to rule in that 140 year cycle.

Roosevelt knew that he was the last to rule in the 144 year progressive cycle of Roman universal influence when he established a new order or new deal idea and broke the Roman order by ruling for 12 years which is the measurement of man. When Roosevelt was giving those famous fireside chats, he knew what was taking place [The beginning of the gradual return of the keys of power to the rightful owners, the Moors]. Everything that was taken from us [Moors] is quietly being prepared for its return to us [Moors]; the gold [The U.S. is tributary to the Moors and they have to repay a 25 million dollars in gold loan that we made to the U.S.: Government in 1861 C.E. that the U.S.: Congress is responsible to repay which is why the seal of the Moors is on the back of the U.S. 1 dollar currency/tender/i.o.u.] and all of the land was taken and so called whites were reduced from landowner status to mere land user status. The land they murdered my ancestors for and stole so that they could fraudulently provide their silent cohorts/their people with fraudulent land grants, land patents, and allodial titles that those thieves and their descendants have no spirtual, moral, or ethical right to [The same applies in Kenya, Zimbabwe, so-called South-africa, Australia, etc.] yet they claim they are a "God fearing nation"… If this is so, the Doctrine of Discovery from the Vatican which is still in force would cease to exist effective immediately. If this is so then the so called whites will gladly return our lands, repay the loan we made to them, make recompense to us for the Tuskegee Experiment, Emmitt Till, Maurice Bishop, The Berlin Conference, and way too much to list here [But don't worry… We will get to that too!!!] to be in harmony with the God the so called "European" claims to love, honor, respect, and obey.

The United:States is bankrupt and its sovereignty is gone. The courts in the U.S. and the States are not solvent thus the Courts and Prosecutors cannot have nor bring a claim against anyone because as a bankrupt entity it has no authority to operate. Therefore the courts in the U.S. and the States cannot and will not resolve any issues. Technically, there are no more courts in the U.S. and the States. There are only private corporations doing business as quasi courts with magistrates and administrative judges (An administrative judge is not the same as a judge).

The U.S.: Bankruptcy is expressed in Franklin-Roosevelts' Executive Order Numbers: 6073,6111, and 6260 (See U.S. Senate Report 93-549 pp. 187, 594) under Trading With The Enemy Act of 1917 codified as United-States-Code: Title: 12: Section: 95a; House Joint Resolution 192 of June 5, 1933 C.E. confirmed in Perry-v-U.S.
(1933), case site 294 U.S. 330-381 and United-States-Code: Title: 31: Sections: 5112 and 5119.

United-States: President: William-J-Clinton and his staff as well as his successors, and the U.S.: Speaker: J-Dennis-Hastert are well aware of the re-emergence of the Moors on the global scene in the form of the **Amexum-Moor-Empire**. All the aforementioned parties know that the day they or their successors return the keys of power to the original legitimate owner, the Moors, is rapidly approaching.

The Amexum-Moor-Empire: National, Regional, and local government is on scene, fully operational, and ready to govern by and under the power, authority, and permission of the Superb and Supreme: Divine-Creator of all things.

United-States: President: William-J-Clinton and his staff as well as his successors, and U.S.: Speaker: J-Dennis-Hastert are well aware of the re-emergence of the Moors on the global scene in the form of the **Amexem-Moor-Empire**. All of the aforementioned parties know that the day they or their successors return the keys of power to the original and legitimate owner, the Moors is rapidly approaching.

The **Amexem-Moor-Empire**: National, Regional, and local government is on scene, fully operational, and ready to govern by and under the power, authority, and permission of the Superb and Supreme: Divine-Creator of all things.

Click On Links Below To See Relevant Documents

(1) Letter Sent To U.S. President Clinton

(2) Letter Sent To U.S. Speaker J. Dennis Hastert

(3) Constructive Notice To U.S. Secretary Of The Treasury

(4) Official Proposal To The Organization Of African Unity

(5) US Bankruptcy Part2

(6) The First TRUE Vietnam

I'm sure most of you all are familiar with the Moors, as pertaining to Noble Drew Ali, the Moorish Science Temple, etc. What's interesting there's a white man by the name of Peter Moon who is acknowledging the Moors and writes about it in several of his books. Here's an excerpt from his book "The Montauk Book Of The Dead"

An excerpt from a chapter in The Montauk Book of the Dead

The Ali Shuffle

At the current time, the door to Moorish mysteries is opening far and wide. The Age of Pisces is at an end, and the Moors are coming to receive their inheritance. Drew Ali instigated this process when he returned to America and released a publication known as the *Circle Seven Koran*. While Drew Ali did not deliver the concise formula as was clearly delineated in *Synchronicity and the Seventh Seal*, he represented the energy and was the energy of such. Drew Ali was very much a part of the mythos and reality that enabled me to write that book. What Drew Ali wrote was geared towards a format that would be accepted by his people at that particular time. It apparently worked quite well.

When the Moorish Science reached its peak in 1929, it was on the heels of one of the greatest, but most dangerous, discoveries Drew Ali ever made. In 1928, Ali attended a Pan American conference in Havana Cuba where he enjoyed broad recognition from a host of other countries. They were, of course, recognizing his sovereign status as a Moorish national who was representing the ancient empire of Amexem. Keep in mind that other countries had no reason to fear Drew Ali or what he represented. It was at this conference, however, that he received a document which was to change the face of Moorish Science forever and would eventually lead to what is known as the Great Schism. That is the name the Moorish community uses to refer to the dispersal of Moorish Science into different groups.

The document Drew Ali received was a copy of a mandate whereby the Amexem Empire extended a land grant of the entire Western Hemisphere to certain Europeans. I have not yet seen the document, and its exact contents are highly mysterious, yet its ramifications literally turned the United States of America upside down. Essentially, it "leased" America to a certain party for a particular number of years, not unlike the way China leased Hong Kong to Great Britain. The lease was up in 2004.

It is entirely reasonable to believe that such a document, if it still exists and can be brought to light, is a mere relic of a long forgotten era that has no significant meaning in today's legal system. That would be fine except for one very important point. If you have truly studied the detailed legal history of the United States of America, you would understand that there is more than a little truth to the prospect of their being such a document. Why? The entire legal history of the United States is predicated on such a proposition.

What is known is that Secretary of State Hughes, from the U.S. Government, attended the Pan American conference and was made privy to this mandate. So were several other heads of state. As a result, a closed-door conference between several nations was held in Geneva, Switzerland and a labyrinthine series of discussions and negotiations began. The Geneva conferences went on for some five years, but records are still kept sealed to this very day. It is known that several international banks called in their loans as a result of this potential legal threat and the stock market crashed in 1929. Several countries, which included the United States, Portugal, France, and Spain, declared bankruptcy in order that relevant powers could buffer themselves from any potential legal claims.

In the case of the United States of America, it was reorganized with a new corporate legal status. Franklin Roosevelt was part and parcel of the entire plan when he abolished the gold standard and created the New Deal. Federal Reserve notes were then issues in place of gold-backed currency. The Great Seal of the Moors was used on the back of the notes.

People behind the Geneva conferences were so concerned about any potential boomerangs from the Moorish issue that they began a full barreled character assination of Moorish heritage. the most flagrant example of this was when two Master Masons put together the infamous *Amos and Andy* show and it became the first nationally syndicated radio show in history. It was deliberately designed to spoof the Moorish Science Temple by lampooning them as the "Mystic Order of the Knights of the Sea" and callously referred to them as sardines. From one perspective, this can be viewed as hysterically funny, especially when you consider that the dignitaries were given titles such as the Swordfish, the Mackeral, and the Kingfish. On the other hand, it was a deliberate and malicious act of intent designed to portray any Moor as the most laughable example of what could be termed the lowest common denominator. Not long after Amos and Andy had its national debut, Drew Ali was arrested and mysteriously died. This has been ignored by both history and conspiracy books. When you see how integrally connected the Moors are to the history of the world, let alone the United States, you see that they are a guidepost to the true history of the planet. this is the lamp of illumination, the Hermit's lamp (from the Tarot), that the secret societies have long played tribute to in their writings.

By reason of our social conditioning, it seems utterly preposterous that the old Moorish Empire could have an actual court-of-law legal claim on this country. Conversely, it appears that world leaders have been deathly afraid of such and have even prepared themselves to legally avoid the inevitable. Once again, the Moors show themselves to be hard-wired into the infrastructure of our consciousness as well as the historical paper trail.

May one thousand seven hundred and eighty four thought proper to constitute John Adams, Benjamin Franklin and Thomas Jefferson their Ministers plenipotentiary giving to them or a majority of them full powers to confer treat and negociate with the Ambassador, Minister or Commissioner of his Majesty the emperor of Morocco concerning a treaty of amity and commerce to make and receive propositions for such treaty and to conclude and sign the same transmitting it to the United States in Congress assembled for their final ratification; and by one other commission bearing date the eleventh day of March one thousand seven hundred and eighty five did further empower the said Ministers plenipotentiary or a majority of them by writing under their hands and seals to appoint such agent in the said business as they might think proper with authority under the directions and instructions of the said ministers to commence and prosecute the said negociations and conferences for the said treaty, provided that the said treaty should be signed by the said Ministers; And whereas the said John Adams and Thomas Jefferson two of the said Ministers plenipotentiary (the said Benjamin Franklin being absent) by writing under the hand and seal of the said John Adams at London October the fifth one thousand seven hundred and eighty five and of the said Thomas Jefferson at Paris October the eleventh of the same year did appoint Thomas Barclay Agent in the business aforesaid giving him the powers therein which by the said second commission they were authorised to give and the said Thomas Barclay in pursuance thereof hath arranged Articles for a treaty of amity and commerce between the United States of America and his Majesty the Emperor of Morocco which Articles written in the Arabic language confirmed by his said Majesty the emperor of Morocco and sealed with his royal seal being translated into the language of the said

Free White Persons. "Free white persons" referred to in Naturalization Act, as amended by Act July 14, 1870, has meaning naturally given to it when first used in 1 Stat. 103, c. 3, meaning all persons belonging to the European races then commonly counted as white, and their descendants, including such descendants, including such descendants in other countries to which they have emigrated.

It includes all European Jews, more or less intermixed with peoples of Celtic, Scandinavian, Teutonic, Iberian Latin, Greek, and Slavic descent. It includes Magyars, Lapps, and Finns, and the Basques and Albanians. It includes the mixed Latin, Celtic-Iberian and **Moorish inhabitants of Spain and Portugal**, the mixed Greek, Latin, Phoenician and North African inhabitants of Sicily, and the mixed Slav and Tarter inhabitants of South Russia. **It does not mean Caucasian race, Aryan race, or Indo-European races, nor the mixed Indo-European, Dravidian, Semitic and Mongolian peoples who inhabit Persia.** A Syrian of Asiatic birth and descent will not be entitled to become a naturalized citizen of the United States as being free white person. Ex parte Shahid D.C.S.C, 6 F. 2d 919, Sk Song, D.C. Cal., 271 F. 23. Nor a native-born Filipino. U.S. v. Javier, 22 F. 2d 879, 880, 57 App. D.C. 303. Nor a native of India who belonged to Hindu race. Kharaiti Ram Samras v. United States, C.C.A. Cal., 125 F.2d 879, 881
. **BLACK'S LAW DICTIONARY, Page 792, Revised Fourth Edition, ST. PAUL. MINN. West Publishing Co, 1986**

Other Titles Available from Califa Media Publishing ™

77 Amazing Facts About the Moors with Complete Proof

"Watch My Prophesies." : An Examination of Prophesies from the Prophet Noble Drew Ali

Holistic Philosophy 101

Moorish Children's Guide to History and Culture

Moorish Jewels: Emerald Ed

Moslem Girls' Training Guide a.k.a. The Sisters' Auxiliary Handbook

Nationality, the Order of the Day

Noble Drew Ali Plenipotentiaries

Official Proclamation of Real Moorish American Nationality

Well, Come to Kianada

Who Stole the Fez, Moors or Shriners?

Califa Uhuru Series

Vol. 1: Holy Koran of the Moorish Holy Temple of Science, Circle 7

Vol. 2: "I'm Going to Repeat Myself.": A Collection of Artifacts Authored by Noble Prophet Drew Ali and the M.S.T. of A.

Vol. 3: Mysteries of the Silent Brotherhood of the East a.ka. The Red Book, a.k.a. Sincerity

Vol. 4: Califa Uhuru; A Collection of Literature from the Moorish Science Temple of America

www.ingramcontent.com/pod-product-compliance
Lightning Source LLC
Chambersburg PA
CBHW030151100526
44592CB00009B/223